T0013559

This accessible book provides the reader with *strategy* in *cognitive* behavior therapy and other evidence-based therapies to lead a meaningful, civically engaged life. The authors explain psychological theories in clear and easy-to-understand terms that will help their audience learn to identify their personal values, develop new skills, and form healthy habits to sustain them through challenges.

—**JUDITH S. BECK, PHD,** PRESIDENT, BECK INSTITUTE FOR COGNITIVE BEHAVIOR THERAPY; CLINICAL PROFESSOR OF PSYCHOLOGY IN PSYCHIATRY, UNIVERSITY OF PENNSYLVANIA, PHILADELPHIA, PA, UNITED STATES

This timely book provides practical, research-tested strategies for the benefit of anyone committed to working to make the world a better place. The authors empathically identify the personal and societal obstacles that can get in the way of sustaining a focus on social justice work but show readers multiple ways to address these obstacles and be effective in living their values.

—**DAVID A. F. HAAGA, PHD,** PROFESSOR OF PSYCHOLOGY, AMERICAN UNIVERSITY, WASHINGTON, DC, UNITED STATES

being
THE
change

being

THE

change

A GUIDE FOR **advocates**
AND **activists** ON STAYING
healthy, **inspired**, AND **driven**

DARA G. FRIEDMAN-WHEELER, PHD
JAMIE S. BODENLOS, PHD

AMERICAN PSYCHOLOGICAL ASSOCIATION

Published by
APA LifeTools
750 First Street, NE
Washington, DC 20002
https://www.apa.org

Order Department
https://www.apa.org/pubs/books
order@apa.org

In the U.K., Europe, Africa, and the Middle East, copies may be ordered from Eurospan
https://www.eurospanbookstore.com/apa
info@eurospangroup.com

Typeset in Sabon by Circle Graphics, Inc., Reisterstown, MD

Printer: Sheridan Books, Chelsea, MI
Cover Designer: Mark Karis

Library of Congress Cataloging-in-Publication Data

Names: Friedman-Wheeler, Dara G., author. | Bodenlos, Jamie S., author.
Title: Being the change : a guide for advocates and activists on staying healthy, inspired, and driven / by Dara G. Friedman-Wheeler and Jamie S.Bodenlos.
Description: Washington, DC : American Psychological Association, [2023] | Includes bibliographical references and index.
Identifiers: LCCN 2022035835 (print) | LCCN 2022035836 (ebook) | ISBN 9781433838002 (paperback) | ISBN 9781433838019 (ebook)
Subjects: LCSH: Change (Psychology) | Social change--Psychological aspects. | Social action--Psychological aspects. | BISAC: SELF-HELP / Personal Growth / Happiness | SELF-HELP / Motivational & Inspirational
Classification: LCC BF637.C4 F75 2023 (print) | LCC BF637.C4 (ebook) | DDC 158.1--dc23/eng/20220909
LC record available at https://lccn.loc.gov/2022035835
LC ebook record available at https://lccn.loc.gov/2022035836

https://doi.org/10.1037/0000330-000

Printed in the United States of America

10 9 8 7 6 5 4 3 2 1

CONTENTS

Contents

ACKNOWLEDGMENTS

We are grateful to so many who have supported us in the writing of this book and in our own justice work. First, we thank Linda McCarter, Stevie Davall, Susan Herman, Laurel Vincenty, and the rest of the team at the American Psychological Association (APA) for orienting us to the APA LifeTools Books editorial process and shepherding this work along. Our reviewers also provided valuable feedback that improved the book substantially. Next, we are so grateful for the many contributions of Nora Ellis, who helped identify resources for the appendix—the Learning More section—and develop the case examples, and who provided consistently helpful and insightful feedback on just about every aspect of the book.

Many thanks to all of our mentors along the way, including Amy Wenzel, who got us into the book world, and Sherry Pagoto, who has inspired us and has supported using our expertise to make the world a better place.

While we can't list all the supervisors, teachers, and mentors who've helped us get to this point, I (Dara) express particular gratitude for the opportunity to have worked with and learned from Dave Haaga and Steve Rao, both role models not just as psychologists but as human beings. Aaron T. Beck, whom I am also lucky enough to call a mentor, has obviously inspired much of this work through his innovations and his own commitment to relieving suffering.

As we mention in the text, social support is a key feature of social action work for many of us. We are grateful to the activists and organizers who have taught us much and to our fellow activists and "helpers" for the work they do, for carrying it forward when we cannot, and for generally making the work more rewarding.

I (Dara) particularly thank my partners in community organizing with the groups Allies for Democracy, Be the Change Bmore [Baltimore], Forge Equity, and Young Successful Leaders, for their leadership, collaboration, and inspiration.

Both of us (Dara and Jamie) thank our families for joining us in this work when possible and for supporting our absences at other times:

> I thank my husband for supporting me emotionally and instrumentally in this work (both the activism and the writing of the book). I could not ask for a more supportive coparent. I also thank my children. I hope the world will be a more just place in your lifetimes—I'm working on it! I am also grateful to my parents who have always been socially and politically engaged and who instilled in me the belief that it is not okay to do nothing while bad things are happening.
>
> —Dara

> I thank my children, Oran and Avery, for always showing love and support to me while I worked on this project. Looking into your eyes every day made me want to make this world a better place. I want to especially thank my husband, Tom, for providing me the space in our lives for my work to right the injustices in the world. Your support of my passions and aspirations helps me keep my own fire burning even during more challenging times. Also, I thank my parents, Bill and Kathy, for always supporting me and showing me that with hard work

and a big heart, anything is possible. And to all of my friends and fellow social justice warriors: Thank you for always inspiring me and making me believe that we can all make a difference in this world.

—Jamie

being
THE
change

STARTING NOW TO CHANGE THE WORLD

How wonderful it is that no one has to wait, but can start right now to gradually change the world!
—Anne Frank (2008, p. 118)

We, Dara and Jamie, the authors of this book, are academic clinical psychologists. We both have always cared about issues—global, societal, and political—that affect us all, and perhaps we were more engaged than some. But it wasn't until a few years ago that we decided to become very intentionally engaged—to think about exactly what level of civic involvement we wanted to have and about how to make that happen. We felt we could help move the needle on social issues we cared about, whether that was through our paid work as clinicians, teachers, and researchers or outside of our day jobs, or both.

We were at stages in our lives in which this seemed tricky: We had young children, full-time jobs, and a host of other commitments. We voted and we kept up with the news, but we weren't sure how to make time for advocacy activities. Fortunately, we realized pretty readily that our training as clinical psychologists and our experience using it to help people with a range of problems came in handy in navigating these challenges. As we supported each other's efforts to engage more deeply in change-making, we found ourselves reminding each other of cognitive behavior therapy strategies, and we had the idea that maybe other people could benefit from these ideas, too. We started with a short column for the newsletter of a professional organization, speaking mainly to others with similar career paths as ours. Based on feedback we received from colleagues who read our column, we now find ourselves here, hoping to share these concepts and techniques with everyone who wants to "be the change" and to maintain some sense of healthy balance in their lives.

You probably recognize the expression "be the change you wish to see in the world," the saying on which the title for this book is based. This quote is often attributed to Mahatma Gandhi, although it turns out there's not much reason to believe he actually said it (Morton, 2011). Nonetheless, many of us seem to take these words to heart, and some dedicate their lives to making things better for future generations through their career paths, through voluntary social and community engagement, or in other ways.

There are many ways to engage in social action (also sometimes called "justice work"), to make the world a better place. This book is intended for readers who want to be engaged in social action or justice work or for readers who want their current work, whether as care providers, organizers, activists, helping professionals, or volunteers, to be more sustainable and to have more of an impact. Many emotional ups and downs come with this work; this book is here to help you navigate them. Whether you are new to social action or have been working on advocacy for decades, this book is for you. It's meant to be a support to help you with various barriers that affect your ability to be effective as you navigate the challenges in making the world a better place.

WHAT IS SOCIAL ACTION?

As you will see throughout this book, we think of *social action* as any efforts aimed at making positive change in society or the world. Some definitions focus on organized efforts and on those that change institutional structures, and we certainly include this type of work in our conceptualization. But we believe there are other ways to make positive social change, too, including work done at the individual level and either at your job or outside of your job. Some of us make positive social change through our careers as schoolteachers, social workers, lawyers, scientists, or nonprofit professionals. Some of us may think of ourselves as activists[1] with respect to issues, such as the environment or civil liberties. But maybe you don't think of yourself as an activist. Perhaps you are making positive change in the world in another way by serving on the Parent–Teacher Association (PTA), being a part of your local rotary club, delivering nutritious meals to people in need via a community-based meal program, participating in a big brother or big sister organization, or infusing an equitable or antiracist perspective into everything you do professionally and personally. Our work could be explicitly political, or it could be aimed more broadly at making positive social change. In other words, this "work" can take many forms.

Efforts that may constitute social action or justice work include the following (this is a noncomprehensive list):

- attending protests
- making phone calls or writing letters or postcards to those in power
- working in politics
- working to influence policy
- working in the public sector or in social services
- working for or with a nonprofit organization
- engaging in community organizing

---

[1]Merriam-Webster (n.d.) defines *activism* as "a doctrine or practice that emphasizes direct vigorous action especially in support of or opposition to one side of a controversial issue." In his book *How to Be an Antiracist*, Ibram X. Kendi defines *activism* more narrowly, saying, "An activist produces power and policy change" (p. 209).

There are myriad ways to make the world a better place. Many people see their entire lives through this lens. They may not be employed by an organization that shares that mission, but they may do their own jobs and conduct their daily lives with that goal in mind. For example, perhaps you work for a bank. You manage a team, and you start your job every day by thinking about how you can make your team members' jobs easier and remove barriers that affect their lives, such as finding good childcare or eldercare. Maybe, at this point, you don't even think about that explicitly. It's just what you've always done. Or maybe you are committed to equity, so you constantly question if your own behaviors, your team members' behaviors, or the practices and policies of the bank are fair to all customers regardless of sex, race, or other characteristics.

Perhaps you are a reading specialist, so your primary job is to teach kids to read, and you do it with the ultimate goal of empowering people to pursue their own dreams. Maybe you see the world through this lens to the degree that you consider the impact of everything you do—from buying coffee to answering your kids' questions about the world—on people in your community or in other countries, or on the earth.

There are all kinds of ways to do this work. You can create an equity committee at your kids' school or in your community. You may be able to take the lead and make changes in the school to help promote an antiracist agenda and enhance diversity in the school district. You might join the PTA or volunteer to lead your kids' scout troop, or, during the winter, you might organize the collection and distribution of hats, scarves, and gloves to people who are currently without housing. You may volunteer to deliver food through a Meals on Wheels program that targets those vulnerable community members who have difficulty leaving their homes to get food.

It may be that our skills can be useful in areas we haven't thought about. For instance, Jamie's friend, Ben, who is opening a jiujitsu studio in her town, has found a way to use this business venture to help the local community. He has partnered with a faculty member at a local university to run a 6-month pilot study to assess how participating in jiujitsu affects use of excessive force and reduces injuries by police officers in the region. Ben is passionate about this topic and hopes that the program will make a difference in the community. Imagine if his study were to reduce the use of force in a handful of police officers. Could that not possibly save a life or prevent an injury that may have occurred otherwise? That is a positive difference in the world with implications well beyond the studio in which the skills are being learned.

Both of us have been active in a number of the ways mentioned earlier as we seek to live our lives through a justice lens. I (Jamie) have volunteered for political campaigns, have been a speaker at several rallies, am involved in advocacy efforts for healthy foods in schools, and have used my classroom and conferences as ways to help people recognize their voice and to increase the dissemination of science through writing and community engagement. In 2020, my family and I delivered meals on Christmas Day through the Rescue Mission. In addition, I have spent my career doing research in underserved communities and continue to publish in this area to help people understand the factors related to health disparities and to better understand their effects.

I (Dara) began my political engagement in 2017, when I started attending protests regularly. Noticing my consistent participation, the organizers of these events reached out to me with other opportunities for political action, and now I am a co-organizer of a local grassroots group, Allies for Democracy. At the same time, I had been advocating for more attention to be paid to racial justice in my local public school, and I ultimately went on to both cofound a neighborhood organization committed to equity and to serve on a PTA diversity, equity, and inclusion committee. More recently, I have sought to make sure that my professional work includes working toward justice. As department chair at Goucher College, I chose to focus my energy on advocating for my department colleagues, particularly my junior colleagues and those from historically minoritized groups, and in my current research, I am working to earn the trust of communities that often are not included in research.

This book focuses on and gives examples of people who either work in a social action-oriented setting or dedicate some of their time outside of work to these activities. We believe that if you are committed to making the world a better place in any way, you will find useful nuggets here to support you in that work, to help you cope with the challenges, and to work toward your goals in more effective and efficient ways. Indeed, this book is intended to make the world a better place by supporting those who are engaged in this work, enabling readers to live more meaningful lives and enabling their work to continue.

EVERYONE HAS A "WHY"

Some of us are motivated to do this work by the injustices we see around us. We may think, "We can do better than this" or "We have to do better than this." Some of the ideas that call us to action may have been with us since childhood. Perhaps we were raised to believe that we should leave the world a better place than we found it. Others may have been taught that when we see bad things happening, we have an obligation to do something. Looking away is not an option. Some may have been working in a job that was not terribly rewarding and started asking, "Could I be working in a field that matters more to me?" or "How can I do work that makes a difference in the world?"

Some of us did not have these messages instilled in us as children but have come to this work as an adult through life experiences that showed us something that is terribly wrong in the world or through an intentional search for meaningful work or for a legacy. Some may have shifted focus after losing a child to gun violence or to a chronic illness, starting a foundation or a lobbying group to address the issue.

Others of us do what we do because we have lived the injustices in our society: We have faced barriers and oppression since childhood. Perhaps you fight for change because your life, or the lives of those in your community, depends on it. If you are a member of a marginalized group, you may well feel that leaving your house every day and the other behaviors that are a part of living your life are, in themselves, acts of resistance or activism. And maybe you've chosen to work more systematically on these issues, too, so that your children and their children can live easier lives or so that you can prevent more unnecessary deaths in your community. Perhaps you are tired of having tackled one barrier only to have another handful of them appear. Or maybe you don't want your grandsons to have to be taught how to "behave" in public so that they are not perceived as a threat.

These are different motivations: Being drawn to justice work to help others is different from doing this work as a fight to survive. We (Dara and Jamie) recognize that feeling compelled to do this work for moral reasons when our own lives are largely fine is a privilege, and we think it's important to acknowledge these different paths toward fighting for a better world.

Feeling that our lives have meaning is what keeps people going. Some of us may not be aware of exactly why we are driven to do the work we do, and it can be helpful to identify where that drive comes from. And some of us once knew why we sought out the work, but the big picture meaning can get lost in the details (or bureaucracy) of this work. We may need to remind ourselves from time to time what the long-term goal is or why the work is personally important to us.

HOW THIS BOOK CAN HELP YOU

Social action work comes with many challenges, both psychological and practical: taking on additional responsibilities on top of an already busy life, needing to organize a group of people with varied goals and ideas (and sometimes challenging personalities), maintaining hope in the face of adversity and suffering, persisting when efforts do not seem to be working, and maintaining physical and emotional safety while doing the work, to name a few. This book addresses these obstacles and others. As you enter or engage more deeply in social action, it's important to have a clear-eyed look at what likely lies ahead in terms of the challenges you will face. We believe it's even more important to know and practice ahead of time how you will respond to or cope with the challenges.

In recent years in the United States, more people have become involved and engaged than they were before. For example, *The New York Times* reported that the Black Lives Matter movement "may be the largest movement in U.S. history" with between 15 million and 26 million people participating in protests following the killing of George Floyd (Buchanan et al., 2020, headline). As more of us deepen or expand our civic engagement and look for tools to help us sustain that action, we are likely to have a range of emotional and interpersonal experiences and challenges. This book is here to support you through those.

We start the book with a topic called "values clarification." We base this part of the book largely on acceptance and commitment therapy. *Values clarification* is the process of making sure you're clear on exactly what it is you care deeply about and about what kind of person you want to be. The next step, of course, is to try to align your daily activities with those values and with your strengths, all the while noticing what brings you joy. This step is important to figuring out how you want to get more engaged or involved. It includes identifying and eliminating activities that take up a lot of time but aren't helping you live a life in accordance with your values as well as finding the space in your life to make these shifts. We also include tips and ideas for getting started, identifying steps you might take to connect with others doing the work you are most interested in.

Some of the challenges in doing this work come from each individual's emotional reactions: When you care deeply about something, you're likely to react to the ups and downs associated with it. Fortunately, this is an area in which cognitive behavior therapy and other evidence-based therapeutic interventions can be helpful in life-changing ways. We therefore dedicate several chapters to managing our emotional reactions, accepting difficult emotions, and taking care of ourselves. Compassion and self-compassion are critical parts of emotion regulation and being effective in your work, so we discuss how to cultivate them in ways that can promote your health and make your work more sustainable.

One of the challenges we discuss throughout the book is related to maximizing your effectiveness in the social action work you are doing. We therefore spend time discussing what is known about how to be most effective in one's work; how to use your strengths to benefit your work; and how to acquire specific new skills that might be helpful, including shifting your mindset, communication skills, and organizational skills. In addition, we recognize that social action work is often done in groups, so we spend time addressing how to work effectively with others as a leader or a team member.

So, how do we keep it going and stay healthy? Certainly, emotional reactions are relevant here, but in the last chapter, we zoom in on strategies for maintaining hope, motivation, and well-being in the long term and in the context of this important work, which itself might evolve over time. We also explore the importance of our social support systems as we try to make changes in the world.

If you are intrigued by any of the strategies or perspectives we introduce in this book, we encourage you to learn more about them! We provide an appendix that includes resources for doing so.

So, here we go. Thank you for picking up this book, and thank you for the work you are doing to make the world a better place. We are right here with you.

CHAPTER 1

TUNING INTO YOUR VALUES AND STRENGTHS

Pivot toward what matters.
—Steven Hayes, founder of acceptance
and commitment therapy (Hayes, 2019, p. 246)

When we feel the urge to get more involved in our communities, many of us have trouble figuring out where to start. Maybe you're at a total loss. Maybe it seems as though there's nothing you can do. You don't know anyone who does this kind of thing, you don't know of any organizations or meetings that are in your area, and you haven't the faintest idea how to find out if there even are any. Or perhaps you know of some opportunities, but you can't quite see yourself getting involved in any of the groups you know about.

Alternatively, you might feel as though there's way too much to do. You get emails from organizations that share your values, and they are always asking for money or time or help or attendance at events. Perhaps when you open these emails you feel like, "Yes! I'll do that!" as though that will be your main focus for this work. But then, the next day, you get an email about something completely different and think, "Oh, I should do that, too!" But there clearly isn't time to do all these things, and you start to feel a bit lost or overwhelmed.

Enter values clarification: When is the last time you sat down and thought about exactly what is most important to you? We build our lives around our priorities, but we may also get swept up in things that seem important because of social pressures but that are, in fact, not what we find most meaningful. In addition to making changes to your daily life based on your values, you can narrow down the possibilities and focus your efforts by considering your personal strengths, your skills (the ones you have and any you might want to learn), your background and experience, and your education and training. In this chapter, we guide you through considering these dimensions and how they might inform your social action work.

VALUES IN ACCEPTANCE AND COMMITMENT THERAPY

Steve Hayes, in his acceptance and commitment therapy (ACT, which is pronounced like the word "act," not like the individual letters "A-C-T"), has developed a number of exercises to help us clarify our values. In ACT, this is part of the "C," the "commitment" piece.[1] What are we committing to? We are committing to living a life consistent with our values. Step 1 is figuring out just what those values are.

Before we explore this first action, let's take a step back. Why are we talking about therapy? It turns out that techniques like acceptance and commitment from ACT and cognitive behavioral techniques from CBT (which we bring up in later chapters) can be instructive, even outside of the therapy setting. We have learned through experience that when we're trying to change our lifestyles to focus more on the issues we care about, the same exercises of acceptance and commitment come in handy.

When we talk about *values*, we are talking about the things you believe to be important in the way you conduct yourself, whether in your work or life or in the way you interact with others. These may be things you learned from your family or in your childhood, either directly, such as being told explicitly that something is important,

---

[1] We discuss the concept of acceptance further in Chapter 4.

or by watching someone engage in behavior in line with a value and internalizing the message inherent in that. Or maybe they are things you realized on your own later in life. Values affect our choices; when we are presented with choices, we often choose the option that is linked to our values. Therefore, values inform the behaviors, decisions, experiences, and events that make up our lives.

You may be thinking, "I know my values; I know what's important to me"—and that's great. Alternatively, you might be thinking, "Um, values? Uh—family? Kindness?" and that's great, too. There are some exercises we can do to help us really hone in what is most important to us and to make those things more concrete and specific as we check to see if our daily activities truly reflect what is most important to us.

For example, one exercise goes like this: Ask yourself, What kind of family member do I want to be? Let's make *that* even more specific: What kind of daughter/father/sibling/aunt/godparent do I want to be?

Next, ask yourself, What does it look like for me to be that kind of godparent (or other family member)? What would I be doing if I were exactly the kind of godparent I wanted to be?

Then would come another question: Am I doing it? If not (or if not always), what gets in the way?

ACT offers a few creative ways to help us tune into our values. Some of these may seem a bit odd to you. The thing is, people often experience values clarification unintentionally—and it's frequently in the context of a difficult situation: a terminal diagnosis, the loss of a loved one. These types of life events sometimes help us see in high relief what is really important to us, what matters most. As one friend put it, while her husband was dying of cancer, "everything else just falls away." What's left is what matters. People often report finding beauty in this clarity. Wouldn't it be great if we could have that sooner in life, intentionally?

In line with this reality, some of the strategies suggested by ACT may seem a bit morbid. One exercise invites you to compose the words you would want on your gravestone (if you were to have a gravestone that said something about you). Other ideas include writing your own eulogy. These can be interesting and illuminating exercises, especially when we get to the step that asks, "Are you living a life consistent with these values?"

Meeting Luke

Consider the example of Luke.[2] Luke is a 28-year-old, White cisgender man who knew since high school that having meaningful work was important to him. When he was growing up, his mother worked tirelessly with children in New York City neighborhoods with high poverty rates. She put in long hours to help these children. Not only was this her career, but it was also where she found meaning. Her whole life, even outside of work, was infused with energy and enthusiasm.

Luke was inspired by her work and her drive to help people. She was a role model to him. In high school, he spent a lot of time volunteering in soup kitchens and after-school centers. Luke values meaningful work that contributes to the community. This is the most important thing to him in the professional domain.

Identifying Your Values

However you go about it, the first step in living a value-driven life is to figure out what your own values are. Perhaps you want to start by just jotting down whatever comes to mind. What is most important

---

[2]The cases used in this chapter and the rest of the book are fictitious, although some are based on real experiences we learned of through our work, through the news, or through the qualitative literature.

to you? Maybe you generate some abstract principles (compassion, people) and some concrete aspects of your life (my family, my friends, basketball). Excellent. We're on our way.

Let's say your list looks something like this:

- justice
- people
- people being healthy
- people being able to be happy

Keep going. What else comes to mind? Just keep writing. Even if some things don't really seem like values or perhaps seem like intrusions into the process (where did "cats" come from?!), keep writing. We can edit and rank and categorize later.

If you're having trouble getting started with a list like this one, you can find existing lists of values online and see which ones resonate with you. The words on the list may be values you hold dear, or they may inspire your own ideas of words or phrases you want to add to the list.

When you're happy with the length of your list, or when the ideas stop coming (kind of like when the popping of the popcorn slows down), you can pause. We say "pause" because you can always add to this list. There's no reason you have to think of everything in one sitting. One thing you can do next is go back and circle the things on your list that you really feel are your core values. Which ones are the most important things to you? Try not to judge—try not to evaluate from the perspective of some outside party. This is not about what your partner or your colleagues or your parents or your Facebook friends would value the most—it's about what *you* value the most. We'll come back to this list.

Next, list the roles you have in life. You could start with a sentence stem like this one: "I am a _____." For example, you might complete that sentence with "daughter, mother, cousin, neighbor, friend, teacher, colleague, mentor, scientist, researcher, psychologist. . . ." According to ACT, there are 10 domains of values: (a) intimate relationships, (b) parenting, (c) family relations, (d) social relationships, (e) careers, (f) education and personal growth, (g) recreation/leisure, (h) spirituality, (i) citizenship, and (j) health/physical well-being. It may be helpful to spend some time thinking about each of these domains. Consider, for example, intimate relationships: This could be about your relationship with your spouse, partner, significant other, or lover. If you are not in an intimate relationship, think about the domain in terms of what you are looking for in such a relationship. Consider the kind of person you are involved with or hope to be involved with. What is important to you in terms of how they act, behave, or relate to others? What is important to you in terms of how *you* behave in these relationships? How do you actually act or behave in the context of an intimate relationship? Which actions are most important to you, and what does that say about you?

The domain of citizenship may be particularly relevant to this book. How would you like to contribute to your community (or communities) or to society as a whole? How do your activities illustrate this value? What do you really want to be "about" in this area in terms of your political, community, and social self? What values do your behaviors demonstrate in these domains? If someone has picked up this book, maybe it's in part because there are some discrepancies here—for example, perhaps we are not doing as much in this domain as we would like; our values don't match up with how we spend our time. Or maybe we are doing *too* much and not really doing it in ways that are satisfying. We will come back to the topic of discrepancies.

Once you list all the core roles or domains (and you do not have to list every last one; consider just listing the ones that seem most key to your identity), it's time to think about what *kind* of a daughter, brother, neighbor, or boss you want to be. For example, I (Dara) want to be a considerate daughter. I'd like to be a dependable and friendly neighbor. I want to be a patient mother. I want to center equity and justice in all of my roles: as a neighbor, citizen, mentor, scientist, and writer. Obviously, you don't have to limit yourself to just one or two adjectives for each role. And you don't have to address every role on the list.

But once we've identified the kind of person we want to be in these domains, perhaps for our top three roles, it's time to evaluate how we're doing right now in terms of these valued directions. Am I, in fact, a considerate daughter? What kinds of things do I do that are considerate? Could I be more considerate of my parents and their needs? Think about the types of things you would do if you were the ideally considerate child. Are you doing most of those? Some of them? None of them?

As we ask ourselves these questions, we want to arrive at a 0-to-10 rating for each of these dimensions, where 0 means *not at all* and 10 means *as much as I would like to be*—that is, a range from "not at all considerate" to "as considerate as I would like to be." You might want to turn your list into a table at this point and place the different values you aspire toward in one column and your 0-to-10 ratings in the next column.

You might be asking yourself what all this has to do with making a difference in the world. After all, being a more considerate daughter might add some pleasantness to my parents' lives and might make me feel a little better about myself, but it doesn't have a huge impact on society. But remember that making an impact on individuals is important, too, and often we can have the biggest, most meaningful impacts on those closest to us. And maybe thinking about what kind of neighbor you want to be *does* align with some of your social engagement goals. Perhaps you want to be the kind of neighbor who makes new neighbors feel welcome, particularly those who might not feel so welcome immediately for various reasons.

However, if all the roles you considered seem more personal than societal, consider putting some other roles into the mix on purpose: What kind of community member/employee do you want to be? Engaged? Involved? The kind of community member or employee who speaks up when they see something wrong? It's also important to think outside the box. We get into habitual ways of thinking, and it's often helpful to consider novel ways to be the kind of person we want to be. Maybe it doesn't look like what we originally envisioned.

For example, let's go back to Luke. He knows that meaningful work is important to him, so in college, he gets his degree in social work. He wants to make a difference in the lives of others and help people who are marginalized. However, after a few years, he starts to find his work unsatisfying and realizes he is doing more paperwork than helping. As he contemplates exploring a new field, he starts to realize just how much his residents look forward to seeing him every day. He is realizing that while the paperwork side of his work is burdensome, he does get to spend a lot of time talking with residents and their families. Sometimes his conversations with residents are the only meaningful interactions they have with another person in a day. Maybe, after all, he is doing the meaningful work he values even if it doesn't "look" the way he originally thought it would.

Paying Attention to Discrepancies

Once we rate ourselves with respect to these values, notice the discrepancies. Perhaps I am "engaged" or "informed" at a 7, and I want to be at a 10. What kinds of things am I not doing (or not doing often)? What are the obstacles that get in the way? Think about the things that are stopping you from getting to a 10. Another question to ask yourself is whether your 10 is actually realistic. How does getting to a 10 in this domain affect your other values? There will probably be some themes. Limited time is a common one: If I were really as considerate a daughter as I'd like to be, I might not have time to be the kind of neighbor I'd like to be. Maybe countermotivation (finding something else more rewarding) is a factor: Maybe I could call my parents every night, but I find that once I get done everything I have to do, I'm exhausted and just want to watch TV. Note these obstacles.

Is this feeling like a lot? Start with one: Pick one value and one obstacle. And think about whether this obstacle or barrier is insurmountable or not. Be thorough and creative here. Don't just assume things are unchangeable. Then look at another—a different obstacle to that same valued direction, or another value and one of its obstacles. Piece by piece; one bite at a time. And remember: Things that are obstacles now might not be forever. You might not need to work two jobs once your kids are grown, for example—and then maybe you'll have a bit more time and energy for these things. You are in a particular phase of your life right now, and things change.

The next chapter offers concrete, practical tips to help you start to address these obstacles and move more intentionally in your valued directions. So, keep your lists and notes handy. For the moment, though, we're going to switch gears and think a bit about our strengths.

YOUR STRENGTHS

For decades, the field of psychology has focused on how to relieve and eliminate human suffering, such as anxiety, depression, and emotional and physical pain. It makes sense that so much energy and time have been put into figuring out ways to ease distress. Indeed, easing suffering may be one of the reasons that you have become interested in changing the world because you see people suffering and hurting. You want to ease others' pain.

Pain and suffering are part of the human experience. Fortunately, so are experiences of joy, happiness, and feeling satisfied. A field of psychology emerged in the late 1990s called positive psychology. The field is just what the term implies: a focus on the positive. One of the positives that came out of this work is a look at strengths. *Strengths* are characteristics that are associated with well-being and quality of life. The strengths are broken down into six categories: (a) wisdom, (b) courage, (c) humanity, (d) justice, (e) temperance, and (f) transcendence (see Table 1.1). There are 24 character strengths described in the field, and you can take the survey to find out what your character strengths are (for the link to the survey, see VIA Institute on Character, n.d.).

Once you know what your strengths are, you can use this knowledge to make the most out of your work to change the world. For instance, when I (Jamie) took the test, my signature character strengths were fairness and forgiveness. How could I use these strengths to improve my work to make a difference in the world? Well, because I discovered that leadership, prudence, and zest were some of the strengths I ranked lower on, it might not make sense for me to take on a leadership role on the committee I'm involved with. However, given that forgiveness and fairness are some of my major strengths, it makes sense that I would advocate for junior faculty in my department and be sure that my junior colleagues have their voices heard in department meetings.

Understanding our strengths will help us thrive and be the best that we can be. More specifically, with respect to our focus in this book, understanding your strengths can also help you be more effective in your desire to make a difference in the world. Does this mean we need to avoid areas that aren't our strengths? Heck no! For instance, even though I (Jamie) scored weaker on leadership,

TABLE 1.1. Character Strengths

Wisdom	Courage	Humanity	Justice	Temperance	Transcendence
Creativity	Bravery	Love	Active citizen	Forgiveness	Appreciation
Curiosity	Persistence	Kindness	Fairness	Humility	Gratitude
Open-mindedness	Integrity	Social intelligence	Leadership	Prudence	Hope
Love of learning	Vitality			Self-regulation	Humor
Perspective and wisdom					Spirituality

Note. © Copyright 2004–2022, VIA Institute on Character. All Rights Reserved. Used with Permission. https://www.viacharacter.org/account/register

I have taken on a few leadership roles over the past few years, and have received feedback indicating I'm effective in those roles, plus I have learned a lot. It's also important to realize that just because something isn't your strength on the test does not mean you cannot grow and work toward improving in those areas (see Chapter 6 for more on going beyond your comfort zone and acquiring new skills).

YOUR SKILLS

You almost definitely have more skills than you realize. I (Dara) often tell my students that my most transferable skill is unjamming photocopiers! It's the one thing I have found handy at every job I've ever had. Do you have a degree in unjamming photocopiers? Probably not. Do you list it on your resume? Again, maybe not. But it's a skill. For me (Jamie), a skill I have that also ties into one of my strengths (social intelligence) is my ability to talk to anyone—and the stranger, the better. Seriously, I could have a 30-minute conversation with a stranger and leave the conversation feeling energized. It makes my spouse feel a little uncomfortable, but that is who I am and what I feel natural doing.

What are you good at? Make a list. Even if it seems like something that's not directly related to the work you might want to do, jot it down. Do you speak multiple languages? Have people always told you you're a good listener? Do you get along well with people from a variety of backgrounds? And don't forget the job-related skills: Do you make awesome PowerPoint presentations or design eye-catching logos and brochures?

Think broadly about your strengths and abilities. You might be surprised at the things you can do that are useful to organizations. Obviously, things like web design and survey design are highly sought after; if you have those skills, organizations might really appreciate your donating them. Data management is also highly useful. Or maybe you have a background in marketing. Do you find yourself receiving messages from organizations and thinking, "Hmm, why did they word it that way?" Perhaps they would benefit from your input.

Or maybe you have a large social network. That, too, is useful when trying to organize. Perhaps, like me (Jamie), you love engaging strangers in conversation or you're great with kids. You might be surprised at what abilities are useful to organizations of all sorts.

These examples might make the most sense in terms of volunteering for a grassroots organization. You might email the organizer and share some of the skills you have.

What about in the context of a job? Perhaps you are looking for a job that makes better use of your skills, or you'd like to shift your responsibilities at your current job in favor of these things. How might you go about this? You could schedule a meeting with your boss or supervisor to discuss shifting your responsibilities. You probably don't want to say, "I think our marketing messages are dumb, and I can do better." But you might say something like, "I think I can contribute to the organization more than I am currently. I don't know if you remember, but my background is in marketing, and I'd love to help with the messaging that we send into the community." Maybe you are an excellent writer and would like to help with grant writing, or perhaps your interpersonal skills might be put to use in networking with potential donors.

List of all of your skills—and we mean *all*. Are you a very efficient dishwasher-loader? Write it down. Are we suggesting you offer to do the dishes for groups you care about? No, not necessarily. But that skill might translate into something else that is of use to your organization. Maybe your agency can't hire someone to help with the enormous workload you and your colleagues have because there's no office space. But maybe there's an office that's being used to store supplies, and perhaps those supplies could go somewhere else if they are just stacked differently (kind of like loading a dishwasher!). Maybe you are good at navigating the intricacies of Zoom or using webinar software, which can be useful for meetings. See where we're going with this?

Obviously, some of these tasks (or their consequences) are more rewarding than others. Don't volunteer to do something you really don't want to do just because you're good at it (unless you think there will be some long-term reward down the road). Be judicious. However, you may also find that a task or position you saw as being "aversive" may be more rewarding than you expect. See if your skills might help you advance your own cause of making a difference.

Maybe while you were making that list, something popped out at you: "Hey, I'll bet that campaign could use someone who understands databases!" or "I wonder if the folks at work know that I have grant-writing experience?" Perhaps some of these skills connect well with your values; maybe you are remembering that you're a good listener, and one of the things you want to work on is being a more helpful neighbor. Excellent. It sounds like you have the beginnings of a plan.

But maybe not, and that's okay. Keep this list handy, too. You may want or need to remind yourself of these skills in conjunction with your values, work opportunities, and many other life circumstances. And update the list as you go. You likely have more skills than you have already noted.

Let's return to Luke again for a moment. Luke had a college friend die by suicide. Afterward, he struggled with how to manage his own feelings and find a way to help his friend's family and loved ones cope. He went through a period of feeling sad and helpless. He wasn't sure what his next steps would be. He didn't know much about suicide or about mental health. Because this area wasn't his strength, he thought about what his strengths were and how to use them to help honor his friend. He knew he was a "people person" (Strength No. 1) and that he was highly organized (Strength No. 2) and was effective in finding resources for people (Strength No. 3; he already does this daily in his own work!).

After finding a suicide support group, Luke met with some other friends and families of people lost to suicide and found a great deal of support. After one of the meetings, he had the idea of organizing a 5K run in honor of his friend with proceeds going to the American Foundation for Suicide Prevention. It was a lot of work, but he was able to use his strengths of organization and working well with others to get it off the ground. He had no problem finding places to sponsor the event because he had lots of connections at different organizations through his job.

YOUR BACKGROUND

"Background" is a pretty broad term, and we're using it broadly here. Your background could refer to your education: Perhaps you're a scientist or an elementary schoolteacher. But it could also refer to your lived experiences: Maybe you know firsthand what it's like to be a transgender teenager in a conservative neighborhood because you had that experience. I (Jamie) come from a family of bricklayers and am a first-generation college student who went on to get a PhD. Think how valuable your experience and understanding could be to those going through similar experiences!

It may be helpful here to do a brief life review: Where were you born? What is notable about your childhood? Your family? Your educational experiences? Places you've lived? What culture(s) do you identify with? Everyone's experience is unique. Think about what aspects of yours you might like to lean into and how you might channel those into your social action work. Notice here that you have agency. For instance, Luke's mother emigrated from Ukraine and had a particular interest in helping refugees settle into their city. The kindness others gave to her when she moved to the United States always warmed her heart, and she wanted to make others feel that way. She volunteered her time at a local church that was responsible for getting refugees' homes set up. She spent weekends going to garage sales to find items that they might need to make their space comfortable. Of course, you may have experienced really difficult things that you don't really want to share with others, or you might not work in a field in which those things are relevant. That's totally fine. There may be ways to make meaning out of those experiences less directly, and there are undoubtedly other ways for you to make a meaningful difference in your world.

YOUR TRAINING

This one may seem obvious, but what were you trained to do? Did you go to school to become a pharmacist? Have you worked for your whole career as a plumber or a photographer? Perhaps you've retired and might enjoy passing along some of your expertise. On the other hand, maybe you're looking for a way to contribute that has nothing to do with your formal training. For some of us, what we do professionally is not really appropriate to also do more casually.

Sometimes we feel frustrated at work when we don't get to use the parts of our training or expertise that we value the most. Are there skills you haven't used in years, or things you learned to do but never got to do professionally? Do you wish you could do them? Identifying these untapped aspects of our training can help us find new avocational projects or make adjustments to our careers to make them more satisfying.

BOTTOM LINE

This chapter is intended to jump-start your thinking about the social action work you do or want to do. In it, we've invited you to do some specific self-reflection that might help you figure out where to begin or how to deepen your engagement.

Of course, the key question might be, Where do you *want* to begin? When you consider your values in conjunction with your strengths, skills, background, and training, what jumps out at you? Where do you see synergy, and more important, what possibilities excite you? In the next chapter, we discuss more concrete ways to pursue these possibilities.

CHAPTER 2

YOUR LIFE AND YOUR VALUED DIRECTIONS

Working toward what one values not only brings a sense of satisfaction but changes what one becomes in the process.
—Albert Bandura (2011, p. 11)

In Chapter 1, we identified some values, strengths, skills, and other characteristics that we bring to the table in our social action work. Our task now is to figure out how we can make our daily lives line up better with our valued directions. Recall what some of these valued directions were (or, of course, check your notes). Bring those to mind as you read this chapter. What do you want to be doing more of? There is almost always room for improvement on this front. Values are aspirational—we don't ever reach them. That's why in acceptance and commitment therapy, we use the term "valued directions"—we are moving in the direction of our values, but we don't ever really expect to get there.

It can be helpful to start by picking one value area that you want to work on. What would work in this area look like? What would you want to achieve? It may help to close your eyes and envision what this would look like and feel like. It may also be helpful to write it down: Write a paragraph or two in the first person and in present tense about what a typical day (or moment) might look like. Can you see yourself in this role? How do you feel doing this work? Are there barriers to getting there? Jot down what you see as barriers; we'll come back to those. It can be helpful to visualize where you want to be, but if it's hard to picture right now, that's okay. It may become easier to visualize later on in the process.

Perhaps you've heard the quote "You are what you do every day"[1] (or similar). The idea is that we are defined by our actions—not necessarily by grand, heroic, once-in-a-lifetime actions but by the activities of our daily lives. But do our days really reflect who we are, or, more important, who we want to be? We may have that feeling, "Where did the day go? I didn't get anything accomplished." Maybe, like many of us, you are spending hours of time scrolling on social media instead of doing activities that are consistent with our values. The first step in this process is figuring out what we are actually doing.

MONITORING

We are going to take an empirical approach to answering that question. By *empirical*, we mean there's an answer out there, and we're going to find it through systematic observation. In other words, let's collect the data. Monitor your time for a week or two. If you feel one week is representative of how you typically live your life, then great. If not, keep going. Include at least one weekend. You may want to make yourself a schedule that looks a bit like a week-at-a-glance calendar (see Table 2.1).

Keep track. Perhaps you'll do this electronically or maybe on paper. You could just keep a running list of times and activities (e.g., "8–8:30: breakfast"). Whatever you like. Ultimately, the question we're trying to answer here is, How are you spending your time?

---

[1]This quote is sometimes (incorrectly) attributed to Aristotle (who did say something similar). Actually, it is an offshoot of something Will Durant (1961) said in *The Story of Philosophy: The Lives and Opinions of the World's Greatest Philosophers of the Western World*: "We are what we repeatedly do" (p. 69).

TABLE 2.1 · Your Week at-a-Glance

Time	Monday	Tuesday	Wednesday	Thursday	Friday	Saturday	Sunday
7 a.m.							
8 a.m.							
9 a.m.							
10 a.m.							
11 a.m.							
12 p.m.							
1 p.m.							
2 p.m.							
3 p.m.							

. . . and so on until your bedtime

Even if you've done this activity before, do it again. There are almost always surprises ("I spend *how long* on YouTube?!") and some new insights to be gleaned. The point is just that: to become more aware of where our time is going and then to make whatever adjustments we can so that we are spending more of our time in ways that align with our valued directions.

So many of us these days are on autopilot. Oftentimes we feel like our time is not our own. We spend our waking hours responding to the demands and needs of others, whether those people are our supervisors, coworkers, children, parents, the people who email or call us . . . the list goes on. Many of us spend a lot of time "reacting" rather than "responding" or consciously choosing how we are spending our time. And maybe we have to. But doing this exercise from time to time can help us to see where there might be small bits of wiggle room—even if just 5 minutes here or there—and to be more intentional about how we spend those moments, which can be really helpful.

For example: Suppose I (Dara) find that I spend almost 2 hours a day on Facebook (it might be beneficial to have an app to track your social media or screen time). Well, perhaps that's because relationships are important to me, and keeping up on my friends' lives is important to me. Or maybe it's because that's where I get my news, and being an informed citizen is one of my values. Heck, sometimes it is a mindless distraction from the chaos of life. Okay, but do I mean to be spending 2 of the 16 hours I'm awake doing those things? Even combined? Would I feel better if I were doing something that had more value to me during that time? Or maybe, on questioning, I feel that there really is nothing more important than maintaining my friendships, and I'm satisfied spending 2 hours a day doing so. That's great.

It's also possible that, in monitoring my time, I discover that I spend almost every evening at my kids' soccer games. Here again,

I want to be a supportive parent, and I love connecting with the other parents on the sidelines. So, it makes sense.

But what happens when a request to do something social action–related comes in—for example, a meeting about forming a diversity, equity, and inclusion committee at my children's school? Do I automatically look at the calendar and say, "Oh, sorry; I can't. We have soccer every night of the week"? Here's where the values clarification work comes in.

Could I miss one soccer game for something that's important to me? Maybe my coparent will be there, so my presence is not essential. Or perhaps another parent could bring my kid and keep an eye on them. Certainly, we want to be there for our kids. But do you also want to create a more just world for your kids—and for all kids? Do you want to show your kids that this work is important and model engagement in social justice work for them?

Maybe being present at every game is really, really important to you. That's totally valid. In that case, take a look at the other activities that are taking up a lot of time. Chances are, work is one of them. And for most of us, that might not be negotiable. But pause and question that just in case. It may well be that you can't work fewer hours. But can you spend your work time differently in ways that line up with your values and passions better? Perhaps you spend a lot of time on administrative work. It's entirely possible you ended up doing certain tasks because you're good at them. But does that mean you *have* to be the one who's doing them? Or could you ask for some assistance with particular tasks (or delegate them to someone else) to free up some time for grant writing, or direct service provision, or whatever it is that you find most meaningful about your job?

Perhaps you notice that you spend *a lot* of time in meetings. Are you the one who calls most of these meetings? Do you need all of them? Could something that is weekly become every-other-week?

Could you work from home, 1 day a week, saving your commute time? For many of us, this may seem more possible now than it did in the past. Thinking of ways to be more efficient with our time can free us up to do other things that are important to us.

Sometimes a seemingly small intervention can make a big difference. Consider email for a minute. This is another task that might take you 5 minutes here, 30 minutes there, 12 minutes there across the day. There are many ways to consolidate this time, as you've probably seen elsewhere, such as picking one time of day to respond to all of your emails (assuming that nothing is urgent). For some people, their energy is lowest at the end of the day, so you could spend an hour in the afternoon, when you have run out of "brain juice," and take care of all of your emails at once. But perhaps you also want to change the *way* you read and respond to email. Maybe, instead of starting with the message that came in first, you start with the message that you think is most likely to connect you with what you find most meaningful in your work and wait on the messages that feel like an energy-suck. Sometimes it turns out that those energy-sucking messages were sent to multiple people, and someone else will respond before you get to it, so you don't have to! Sometimes you have to. But it is possible that this strategy will result in having more time for more meaningful activities in your day.

EVALUATING YOUR DAYS

Once you've completed your monitoring, do some adding. How much time are you spending per day, on average, on the various activities that make up your daily life? You might end up with something that looks like this:

- Meal preparation/eating/cleanup: 2½ hours
- Parenting: 4 hours

- Commute: 1½ hours
- Work: 8 hours
  - Email: 1½ hours
  - Teaching: 5½ hours
  - Grading/preparation: 2 hours
  - Meetings: 45 minutes
- TV: 2 hours
- Social media: 1½ hours

Now, take out your notes about your values. Are they reflected in this day? Hopefully, many of them are. Chances are you're pretty invested in your role as a parent, if you are one, and you want to be a good employee, so it makes sense that these domains take up so much of your day. That's pretty great (and realizing that these things are aligned may help you to appreciate the various tasks that fall into these categories). But maybe you also want to be a more active participant in the community engagement group at your church, and you don't see any time dedicated to that. What do you think would be the ideal amount of time to dedicate toward that valued direction?

Perhaps you think, "Wow, I really want to get more involved with that group. I can't believe I haven't been to a meeting in weeks!" You realize that being a part of this group is an important part of how you think about yourself and what kind of person you are, but your daily life doesn't reflect that. Maybe this isn't something you are going to fit into every week, but you want to aim to go to at least one meeting per month. Or maybe you'll do more in the summer or winter and less in the other seasons.

Many of us have a lot of responsibilities, and it's not easy to see where we might find more time. Sometimes some of our responsibilities (e.g., work) squeeze out other valued activities (e.g., quality time with children). Some of us have jobs that are theoretically 9 to 5, regular business hours, Monday through Friday, and yet we do work in the evenings and on weekends. Perhaps you're thinking, "No, I never bring work home," or you never sit down at your desk on the weekends to dive into a project. But do you answer work emails on your phone from wherever you are? Do you find yourself telling your family or friends, "Hang on, let me just take care of this one thing . . ."?

Maybe you do those things and feel like it's totally appropriate (in which case, you may be feeling a bit annoyed with us for suggesting otherwise). If this is what works for you, by all means, stick with it! We're just encouraging folks to take a look at these things, to be aware of them, and to be intentional about them. So, if it works for you, great. But if it doesn't, if you feel like it's not strictly necessary for you to respond to those emails outside of work time, or if you feel like you're constantly telling your kids to "hang on," you can make different choices. Maybe you can take your work email account off your phone (and ask your colleagues not to text you on your personal phone for work-related matters). If you can't get rid of your work email on your phone, consider putting it in a folder called "work" on your last screen of apps so that you have to be very intentional in selecting it. Just building in this kind of pause can, well, give you pause. You might find—as you're looking for or accessing the app—that you don't actually need to do so right at that moment, and you might shut off your phone and be present for the people who are physically around you.

For some of us, it might be impossible to make adjustments right now. We get that. If that's the case, table it. In these situations, we might want to think about using our time more intentionally as more of a long-term quest. But let's not defer this activity until we're really sure we've exhausted all possibilities and there is no wiggle room. If we can make even small adjustments now, let's do it.

SETTING GOALS

Consider the example of wanting to participate more in the community engagement group at church. How much time would you feel good dedicating to this group and to this valued direction? Perhaps you have thought, "Well, I should be able to spend at least an hour a week on this!" (Be aware of "should" statements. We'll come back to those in Chapter 3.) But let's say that's what feels best for you— at least an hour a week.

You look at your schedule, and you see that at the time the group meets, you're now picking up your teenager, Terry, from their job. Hmm. That one's tricky. Is there any other way for them to get home? Could they take a bus? Ask a coworker for a ride? If you're not sure, you could plan to talk to your teen about it when they come home from school. In the meantime, is there anything else you could do to connect with this group and their work more? Could you email the group contact and double-check the meeting time, and let them know that you're trying to work something out so you can attend the meetings but also ask if there are other ways you can help out? Perhaps you can attend their events or activities, even if you can't go to the meetings. Or you could prepare materials at home on your own time. Explore the options.

What do you notice about this example? We're illustrating several aspects of effective goal-setting practices. For one thing, we're being very, very concrete. We went from an abstract goal (participating more in the community engagement group) to specific activities (emailing the group leader, planning to attend meetings). None of these are "be more involved" kinds of goals. They are too vague. We want something that is concrete and measurable so that at the end of the week or month, we will know if we're moving toward our goals. Next, as we noted earlier, we started small (sending an email, problem-solving with the teenager). This is part of effective goal setting, too, often referred to as "set(ting) yourself up for success": Set goals you can reach. It doesn't mean you're not being ambitious or that you can't do more. It means that we know, from research, that making changes gradually increases your likelihood of successful, sustained change.

So perhaps as a first step, you have these conversations, and then after a while, your teenager's work hours change, or they discover there's a bus stop not too far away, and you realize you can attend the meetings, so you add those in.

But maybe this is a really busy time at work, and you spend every free moment catching up on the things you don't get to during the week like laundry and grocery shopping and errands. That idea of adding in the meetings seems overwhelming, but you really want to be a part of things. That's okay. This is where the short- and long-term goals come in. Perhaps, for now, you stick with whatever group tasks or activities you can fit in, but you make a note of the meeting time in your calendar for a time when you think things will be a little calmer, maybe in a month or so. The goal is to make this work fit into your life in a way that is sustainable.

MAKING ACTION PLANS

Changing our habits is hard, as most of us have discovered by the time we get to adulthood. Research has found that we are more likely to do things when we have what are called *implementation intentions*, that is, detailed plans of how we will carry out a behavior. How will we implement this change? In cognitive behavior therapy, we think of these as "action plans." Again, notice the language: We've gone from abstract values to concrete action plans. We're making things happen.

An important part of implementation intentions is scheduling a specific time for a particular activity. Don't just say to yourself, "I'm going to do something related to community engagement this week" or "I'm going to start attending meetings when Terry's work schedule changes." Make it an appointment in your calendar like the other things you prioritize. Make a plan to attend the meeting scheduled in late April. Set a reminder in your phone not just right before the meeting but a few days before it so you can figure out if you need to move anything around so you can go. Technology can be really helpful here (e.g., you can set reminders on your phone). No matter how you do it, good plans are typically concrete and measurable. A plan that is *concrete* is specific enough that you know exactly what you need to do to implement it. A plan that is *measurable* provides a way for you to assess afterward if you did it or not.

Sometimes the easiest way to see what these terms mean is by looking at counterexamples, or plans that are not concrete and measurable. "I will start going to meetings again when Terry's work schedule changes" is probably measurable (you'd know if you went to the meeting or not), but it's not concrete enough. It doesn't tell you exactly when you're going to do it or for how long. A plan that was neither concrete nor measurable might be: "I'm going to incorporate more community engagement into my life." How? When? What will that look like? How will you know if you've done it or not? Sometimes asking yourself these questions can help you develop a plan that is concrete and measurable.

One strategy that can help a lot of people reach their goals is *social accountability*—that is, announce your specific goal publicly. This can be a very effective strategy to help achieve your goals. You can do this in many ways, and you don't have to shout it from a rooftop. You can just tell family and friends. You may find that telling your mom that you're going to start attending community engagement meetings makes it more likely that you'll do so, knowing she might ask you about it at some point. Perhaps you start a text chain with your friends, sharing your goal and inviting them to do the same, or share it on social media to recruit others. These activities can add a layer of meaning to the activity itself and can help you stay on track. A few more resources can help you make plans that work: See the appendix in this book and look under "Productivity" and also "Physical Activity," topics to which these ideas are often applied.

MANAGING TIME

Some of us have more flexibility in our lives than others, and we may have more flexibility at different times in our lives than at other times. We (Dara and Jamie) have noticed that, in some of our social action work, we are among the youngest people in the room. Many of the people present have retired, which might make it easier for them to fit in some of these activities. It can be hard to fit everything in, and we want to make sure we're not doing too much and running ourselves ragged. But for many of us, we can adjust some small things in our day that will help us to shift the balance of doing things we *have* to do and to doing things that are *meaningful* to us and that move us toward our valued directions. In other words, maybe you can subtract some things to make room for the things you want to add.

For example, do you do all the meal prep and cleanup in your house? Do you have a partner who could do more? Or is one of your kids now old enough to do more? Some people suggest that kids can start making dinner for the family at age 10! Many of us are probably thinking, "Oh, holy cow, that's just what I need right now—to find the time to teach my 10-year-old to cook!" Right. It involves some time up front, and maybe this is not the exact moment. But that investment of time up front could liberate time for you down the road.

Maybe it's a roommate or partner who could be doing more, and maybe it's hard to bring that up for various reasons. See if it helps to remind yourself that you could be using the time that would be "freed up" toward a greater good if your roommate or partner were to pick up a little of the slack. You might want to refer to Chapter 5 on intentional communication as you plan a conversation on this topic. (It might also be worth remembering that most people think they do more around the house than their partner. If you add up the estimates each person in a relationship gives, of how much they do, it often totals more than 100%! So, you might want to go into any conversations on the topic remembering that your view might not be the same as the other person's.)

Perhaps that particular example doesn't make sense in your life. Lots of other life hacks can help you increase the amount of time you have to dedicate to living a life consistent with your values. Consider what your actual day looks like in terms of the time you wake up and go to sleep. Are you getting caught up on movies or binge-watching Netflix in the evening and sleeping in late? Could you set concrete bedtimes and wake times for yourself so that you have more time to do activities that are important to you? What about email, as mentioned before? Could you change the way you handle email and save yourself some time?

There are many ideas out there for "containing" the amount of time and energy you spend reading and responding to email, including those mentioned earlier. Do a quick Google search and see if any of them seems worth trying. Even just the smallest intervention (e.g., signing out of your email at the end of each workday as opposed to leaving it open) can make a difference. I (Dara) have a colleague who found that setting an out-of-office reply *on* the weekend was liberating, even though in her line of work there was no reason she *would* reply to email on the weekends. Some of these interventions are small enough that they're worth trying even if, at first, they don't seem like they'd make a difference. In all seriousness, what do you have to lose? Test them out. The worst-case scenario is that you tried, and it doesn't work, which just means you have to try something else.

Let's look at some other work-related examples.

Where do you think you "lose" the most time during the day? If you monitored your time in a detailed enough way, this may become obvious to you. And if not, you can always take a few days and monitor your time more closely (use a schedule grid like the one we presented earlier in the chapter; see Table 2.1). Perhaps, if you are retired, it is chatting with neighbors or doing things around the house. Have you established a routine that makes it difficult to find time to fit in community service work? What do *you* find most meaningful? Are there things that matter less that could wait while you focus on the things that make the most difference?

If you work and have a door to your office, maybe you could close the door more often. Shut off your phone or close out of your email. Let your coworkers know that you need to focus on something in that moment. (There are nice ways to do this, by the way, like saying, "Let me get through these files, and then I can chat.") Having your own office space may not be your reality, but are there other ways to manage your time that could help? Sometimes it requires thinking outside of the box. Maybe you can't make yourself unavailable at work. Maybe being available to your clients, colleagues, or customers is key to what you do. Okay, then let's look elsewhere. What about meetings? We talk more about meeting efficiency in Chapter 7.

Another strategy that can help you align your daily life with your values is to practice mindfulness. Do you ever feel that you are having difficulty really getting into a task because you are overwhelmed by your busy mind? By taking time out of your day to practice short, breath-focused meditations, you are not only getting in touch with the moment (which has many benefits) but you are also strengthening your ability to concentrate and be efficient at work. We live in a world that is full of distractions, and it's often difficult to be present in the moment. Indeed, we may be trying to work and be thinking about a whole host of other things that we need to do at home, or something that bothered us on social media, or concern over a loved one who is having a troubling time. It may also be that our own emotions are overwhelming us, and our thoughts about those emotions are disrupting our ability to focus at work. The more we are actually present in the moment, the better we can attend to the task at hand. Practicing mindfulness can be beneficial to giving us some perspective and room between our tasks and the busyness of our minds. That "space" is often what we need to be aware of our intentions and to take action toward living a more meaningful life. We discuss mindfulness further in Chapter 4.

Be creative here about where you might be able to increase your efficiency or productivity. Remember Luke from Chapter 1? He became a social worker to help people and then ended up spending much of his time on paperwork. While the heavy paperwork burden many people experience in their fields may not end anytime soon, perhaps the way it is managed could be addressed. Maybe Luke could consider the timing of his paperwork and try to tackle it in the afternoons when he has less face time with residents and more uninterrupted free time to spend at his computer. Sometimes even a small change can make a big difference.

This dissonance may also lead Luke to second guess or question his career path. He may find that the role he is currently in is not what he wants to do long term, and maybe he starts to look at other jobs in the social work field that will allow him more time to work one-on-one with people.

FINDING A NICHE

We talk about wanting to get more involved in a group you're already aware of or finding ways to feel more satisfied at work. But what if you have (or have made) the time you need to do this work, but you aren't sure exactly where to put that time and energy? Perhaps you've never really done anything like this before and aren't sure where to begin. Often it makes sense to start with your own community. Doing so can take a number of forms. Maybe this means you look for opportunities associated with your faith community, or you look to see how you can help in your local city or town. Or you could ask a friend or a family member who is active in this kind of work what groups they know about.

Are there activities you are already involved in where you could be more involved? It could start as simply as keeping an eye out for your older neighbor. You notice it's hard for them to get groceries on their own, and they have no family, so you start picking food up for them. Over time, you notice a trend with other older adults who live near you who struggle without community help. That could lead you to look into local service organizations. Maybe in making that connection for your neighbors, it leads you to want to get more involved because the poverty in your neighborhood is being overlooked by elected officials. Things come to a head when you go to check on your neighbor in the dead of winter and find that their heat was shut off and that your neighbor has been living in frigid conditions for the past few days. Pretty soon, you find yourself running for a seat on the city council because what has happened to your neighborhood is not okay with you, and you see that if you don't work toward change, who will? What will happen to all of the neighbors with no one looking out for them?

Not everyone will go from the occasional grocery pickup for a neighbor to running for city council. We will all connect the dots differently. In the scenario just described, for example, another person might not run for city council themselves but instead use their connections and resources to boost leadership capacity among other potential spokespersons and "champions" in their community.

We can use our unique combinations of values, strengths, skills, background, and training to find the best ways to plug in.

You can take action at multiple levels. You can work at the individual level, the community level, or the broader systems level, as the earlier scenario illustrates. What are some other examples of what different "levels" of social action might look like? Well, at the individual level, perhaps you might get involved in raising awareness about an issue, whether it's a political issue or a health issue or something else that's important to you. Canvassing and phone banking operate at the individual level because you're having one-on-one conversations. Casual conversations with friends and neighbors also can lead to change. At the community level, you might be more involved in something associated with an institution, such as your neighborhood association or the PTA. Maybe you work with others to get one of those groups to take up a particular issue. Or maybe you want to take on an even bigger systems issue having to do with a law or policy.

As another example, suppose that while you were waiting in line to vote during the last election, you witnessed the difficulties that people in wheelchairs had in accessing and using the polling place. It got you thinking that it must be a challenge for people with disabilities to have access to voting. When you went home that night, you looked up the statistics and found that a relatively smaller number of disabled people register to vote, and they vote at lower rates than nondisabled people. What do you do with this information? How do you effect change on such a large scale? Well, a good first step could be looking into the Americans With Disabilities Act of 1990 and how voting rights and accessibility are discussed. From there, it may be that you reach out to The American Association of People With Disabilities and see if there are ways that you can help. Often organizations such as this one are a great place to get more information and find avenues for involvement.

Again, sometimes we can have the most impact when we start with our own communities. Your neighbors may be more persuaded by what you have to say because they know you live in the neighborhood. Consider starting where you have or could easily make personal relationships. Like the example about disabilities and voting just mentioned, sometimes you become aware of a major societal issue because you see it playing out in your own community. Wouldn't it be nice to see changes that benefit those around you? A tangible change that you can see is reinforcing. However, this doesn't mean you can't help people or causes in other parts of the world or that you can't start working at the broader policy level. You can. You can have an impact at any or all of these levels. And, of course, they are interrelated. Who makes policies? Humans. Who composes cultures and institutions? Again, humans. Whatever level you work at will have ripple effects on the others.

HANDLING OBSTACLES

For some of us, the main obstacle to being an advocate is daily fatigue because our own lives are affected by barriers to access or barriers to getting ahead. We want to lift up others, but most days, we're just keeping our own heads above water. For others (like us, Dara and Jamie), most systems have served us well. We are able to get an education and health care, and we can take part in elections.

Whatever our circumstances, there will be barriers along the way to living a life that is totally consistent with your values. These may be things that you do not anticipate. It's important to be aware of these barriers but also to know that encountering barriers is the norm, not the exception. If we realize that obstacles will come up, we are more likely to treat them as temporary. This is where we can practice being flexible in the way we approach the situation and also ask questions in a kind, gentle manner about what got us off track.

Don't beat yourself up if things end up sliding a bit. Look at the situation from a position of curiosity instead of judgment. Take a step back from the situation and ask yourself how you got off track and what you can do to get back on track. You may find it helpful to use the problem-solving approach outlined in Chapter 7.

Life is full of challenges and stressors. As we hear so often, this is a marathon and not a sprint, and using strategies in this book will help us stay in it for the long haul.

BOTTOM LINE

Finding ways to make your life "match up" better with your valued directions does not have to mean making huge changes to your life (although it could!). There may be small interventions you can use or changes you can make to your daily routine, at home and at work, that may free up time for you to spend more intentionally in ways that move you toward your valued directions.

Many of us are very busy, and there may not be much wiggle room in your day, but we strongly encourage you to consider the strategies described in this chapter to see if you can make even a small adjustment that may increase the meaning you find in your day-to-day life. See if you can set aside your skepticism and try some things out. You may be surprised at how liberating these microstrategies can be!

CHAPTER 3

MANAGING EMOTIONS: COGNITIVE REAPPRAISAL

The greatest discovery of my generation is that human beings can alter their lives by altering their attitudes of mind.
—William James (1890, p. 290)

Like so many things in life, social action work can inspire many different emotions. Because this work tends to be motivated by passion or our own personal experience of trauma or discrimination, it may lead to varied and intense emotions. Whether you are just starting out or have been involved for a long time, take a moment to think about what motivated you to get involved in social action work. Perhaps it was a sense of moral duty or obligation, a strong belief that something in the world needed changing, or both. Maybe you have a passion for working with people, advocating for people, helping them solve problems, watching them master something new, or just being present and supportive in times of crisis. It could also be a matter of survival for you. For many of us, just being ourselves in this world is itself an act of resistance. Our life experiences can drive us in the work that we do.

MARCELLA'S STORY

In this chapter, we meet Marcella, a 37-year-old, cisgender Latina woman from Michigan who works at a nonprofit. Marcella is an avid proponent of increased access to health care, among other issues. She grew up not going to the doctor much; no one in her family did, except in a crisis. She lost her father to diabetes, which she later learned probably would have been treatable if he had had access to the care he needed. Whenever she hears about people not getting the care they need, she feels her heart race and her shoulders tense. Marcella is determined that other families not experience preventable losses like hers.

Marcella's story reflects how she came to this work. Take a few minutes to reflect on how you got to this place of wanting to make a change in the world, whether you are already doing the work or you want to get started. What drew you to it? What did you hope to accomplish when you got started on this path? It may be helpful to write these things down. It's easy to lose sight of that initial urge and passion, so take some time with this step. If you find it's easier to remember feelings than thoughts, write about those.

Let's focus on those feelings for a moment. Did you feel excited, confident, frustrated, sad, energized, angry, driven, indignant, scared . . .? Perhaps you felt several of those or something entirely different. Probably in the time since that moment, you've felt a whole slew of emotions related to your social action work. Perhaps you came back from a rally feeling hopeful or motivated or excited. Maybe you arrived at work one day to discover the budget had been cut for something you cared deeply about and had worked hard on, and you felt demoralized. Perhaps you woke up one morning to hear election returns that disappointed you—all the more so if you'd been putting in hours canvassing or making phone calls to get your preferred candidate elected, or if you are afraid the person who won will cause direct harm to you or your loved ones. Maybe you're angry that a student in your class who is experiencing food insecurity just had their family's Supplemental Nutrition Assistance Program benefits (commonly known as SNAP or food stamps) taken away or had to drop out of school.

Do all of these feelings need "managing"? Not necessarily. Indeed, acceptance and commitment therapy (ACT) encourages us *not* to try to change our feelings on the premise that trying to change or avoid them is the source of many life problems and of our own distress. Often, the effort and energy we put toward trying to rid ourselves of negative emotions takes away from living a life consistent with our values (as addressed in Chapters 1 and 2). We come back to ACT's perspective on emotions in the next chapter.

But might you sometimes want to try to adjust your emotions a bit? Turn down the volume on them? Or perhaps you believe in letting them have their life and don't want to change them, but you want to find a way for them to impact your behavior (including your sleep!) a bit less.

Enter mood management techniques. When was the last time you felt something uncomfortable and wanted to change it? This may be easy; perhaps it was today—or perhaps it was last week.

Let's look at an example related to activism. Marcella, whom we just met, is an enthusiastic activist who generally finds her efforts (like protests and canvassing) to be invigorating. Yet she has gone through periods in which she lacked the motivation to take any action. She sees the social media posts and the emails asking her to write, call, show up, or canvass, and she has the thought "What's the point?" or "Stop asking me to do stuff!" She sometimes finds herself feeling hopeless. We're not going to argue about whether that feeling is justified, but it may well be getting in the way of her goals and valued directions. Instead, let's think about how Marcella might respond to it and *keep moving* in her valued directions. We're going to start by exploring the cognitive model, the basis for many cognitive behavior therapy approaches. We then take a close look at one such approach: cognitive reappraisal. In the next chapter, we discuss other approaches to these emotions.

THE COGNITIVE MODEL

The cognitive model suggests that four aspects of our psychological makeup are interrelated: our cognitions or thoughts, our emotions, our behaviors, and our physiological reactions.[1] According to the cognitive model, each of these influences all the others. In other words, our cognitions influence our emotions, behaviors, and physiological reactions—such as when worry causes you to feel increased anxiety (emotion), to avoid whatever you're worried about (behavior), and to lose sleep (physiological). Our emotions affect our thoughts, behaviors, and physiological reactions, and so on, as depicted in Figure 3.1. Sometimes the environment is included

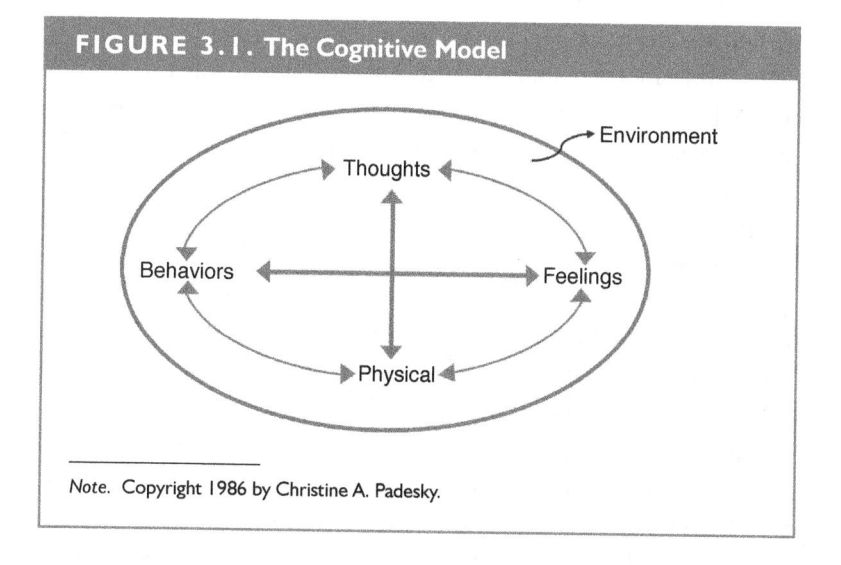

FIGURE 3.1. The Cognitive Model

Note. Copyright 1986 by Christine A. Padesky.

[1]Sometimes physiological reactions are lumped in together with "behaviors," which is defined broadly. We think it is sometimes helpful to consider physiological reactions, such as a racing heart, separately from our more overt behaviors.

in this model as the context in which all of these things happen (and a factor that influences them, too).

The idea that these things influence each other has a lot of research support. It also provides us with a variety of ways of "intervening," or taking care of ourselves, when we experience psychological distress. For example, if we are having difficulty sleeping, we can look to see if there are thoughts (worry about work), emotions (anxiety), or behaviors (drinking caffeine right up until bedtime) that might be contributing to this problem. Maybe caffeine is the easiest thing to tackle, so we try that first.

Let's look at Marcella's situation from this perspective: The behavior in question (that is not in line with her values) is her withdrawing from her social action work. What other factors may be influencing that? Well, we saw earlier that she was having thoughts like "What's the point?" It certainly makes sense that if you see no point, you're not going to do something. Perhaps that thought also gives rise to a feeling of sadness or despair. These feelings are also not likely to lead directly to action. Perhaps she feels muscle tension when she thinks about going to one of these events or participating in an action. Again, when we break her reactions down this way, it makes perfect sense that she is not participating in these activities.

Cognitive reappraisal tackles the effects of thoughts on our reactions more directly as though we are "zooming in" on that part of the model. You can also think of the process as something like this:

situation → thoughts → reactions

This version of the model does a couple of things. For one thing, it explicitly includes the "situation," which is represented as the environment "oval" in the model shown in Figure 3.1. It also combines feelings, behaviors, and physiological reactions under one element: reactions. For another visual of this model, see Beck Institute (n.d.).

"APPRAISING" YOUR THOUGHTS

When we zoom in on the thoughts we are having, and on their effects, we do so to see if we might be able to adjust our thoughts a bit so that our reactions are more in line with our values. This is an approach called *cognitive reappraisal*, or, in the context of cognitive behavior therapy, *cognitive restructuring*. Often we feel the way we feel and do the things we do because of the thoughts or appraisals we have about a given situation. In other words, although we mostly walk around thinking it's all the stressful situations in our lives that cause our unhappiness, cognitive theory holds that our *reactions* to our situations—in particular, our thoughts about our situations—contribute greatly to unhappiness. Of course, some situations are stressful regardless of how you think about or react to them. If you are worried about how you will buy food to feed your family for dinner tonight, we are not suggesting that you could just think about the situation differently and find it to be nonstressful. We do not mean to minimize the very real struggles that cause very real distress, as an extreme interpretation of cognitive theory might seem to do. But sometimes the amount of distress caused by even objectively stressful situations can be reduced a little by choosing where we focus our thinking.

For example, perhaps you really like the focus of the policy center you work for, but you feel frustrated, repeatedly, by their inefficiency. Elsewhere in the book, we talk about ways you can work with others to make your (collaborative) work more efficient, but let's suppose that for now, you've done what you think you can do, and you're just trying to figure out how to deal with the slow pace or inefficiency of the work without it causing an increase in your irritability or frustration.

What kinds of thoughts are you having when you notice you're getting irritated? For example, are you thinking things like this: "Ugh, there he goes again. He just talks and talks and talks every week without ever saying anything." Or are you thinking, "Why don't people understand how to run a meeting?!" or "This is a waste of time!"

These thoughts (and a host of others that lead to irritation, frustration, or anger) have something in common: They assume that things *should be another way*. The person in the example *shouldn't* talk and talk and talk. And people *should* know how to run meetings.

Well, maybe. It would be nice. But it's not the way things are. And really, why should the world conform to our preferences? Perhaps the man really needs to talk. Perhaps he doesn't have anyone else to talk to about these things, and he really needs the validation and social support from like-minded folks. Perhaps he works things out in his head by talking about them with others. Are those goals less valid than "having an efficient meeting"?

These kinds of questions are one way you might examine the thoughts that seem to be leading to your negative feelings. While it's true that many people find long meetings to be frustrating, some people probably get more upset about them than others, and the idea here is that, at least in part, those differences in emotional reactions might be the result of the thoughts or interpretations we have about the situation (in this case, long meetings). Noticing and evaluating these thoughts are two steps of cognitive reappraisal, which we'll walk through more systematically now.

Notice Your Thoughts

The first step in cognitive reappraisal is noticing your thoughts. Aaron T. Beck, the founder of cognitive therapy, called these *automatic thoughts*, the thoughts that run through our heads in such a habitual, automatic way that we may not even be aware of them. They're involuntary and sometimes happen outside of our consciousness, like the steps of brushing our teeth. You likely brush your teeth twice a day, but you probably do not stop every time and think consciously, "I need to pick up my toothbrush. Now, I need to turn on the water and wet my toothbrush. Next, I will turn off the water and pick up the toothpaste." But you're doing those things anyway.

Automatic thoughts are like that. They happen whether we're paying attention or not. And the idea behind cognitive reappraisal is that those thoughts, even if we're not aware of them, affect us. They influence our behaviors, they might influence our physiological functioning (interfering with sleep or making it hard to sit still), and they influence our feelings.

So, our goal here is to see if we can identify and then perhaps adjust some of those automatic thoughts so that we end up with different reactions, or perhaps just a less intense version of the emotion that's bothering us.

How can we become aware of these thoughts? Well, there are a few tricks. The first is to notice when the emotion comes up for you. Perhaps you got mad when a colleague made an offhand comment that you found insulting. The question you want to ask yourself is, "What went through my head right then?" Remember: According to this theory, it's not just the colleague's comment that makes you mad but also the thoughts you have in response to it. This doesn't mean that your colleague is not to blame or that you are to blame. It just gives us a way to address how we feel.

See if you notice some words or perhaps an image that accompanied or came right before that anger. Maybe something like these: "People are so self-centered!" or "Why am I the only one doing something about this?" Or maybe you have an image in your head of yourself standing alone as everyone else drives off to do their own thing.

Cognitive reappraisal can take a couple of forms. One is evaluating whether our automatic thoughts were accurate or rational. And that may be useful in some situations. But sometimes your thoughts may be perfectly rational and still give rise to emotions that are not helping you get where you want to go. So, we prefer to focus on whether thoughts might be "dysfunctional" or "unhelpful."

Are you the *only* one doing something about the situation? Probably not, in most cases. Regardless, is it helpful to think about it this way? Or might there be other ways of thinking about it that might let you get over your irritation with your colleague's cavalier attitude more quickly and think of productive ways to make the situation better? If you find a more helpful way to think about things, write it down. Put it on a sticky note, or set an alarm on your phone to remind you of this more helpful thought.

To see how this can work in practice, let's come back to Marcella. Marcella has been canvassing for a candidate she *really* wants to win. It's election night, and she is continually hitting refresh on her computer as the returns come in. It's looking worse and worse. It gets to be midnight, and it's still not entirely clear who's going to win, but it looks pretty bad for her candidate. She decides to go to bed so that she is not too exhausted in the morning, but she is mad. She tosses and turns instead of sleeping.

First (and this is often the easiest part), identify the situation. For Marcella, that would be the fact that the candidate she canvassed for is likely to lose.

Next, she needs to identify the automatic thought that she had. To do this, she can try to rewind to the moment she noticed she was angry and ask herself, "What was going through my head?" Maybe she would find she was thinking, "It's no use," or "Why do I waste my time?" or "I can't believe there are this many idiots who voted for the other guy."

Let's take a look at the first of these thoughts: "It's no use." Once we've identified a thought to work with (to reappraise), we then identify the emotions. Sometimes the emotions are not entirely obvious to us, either: Sometimes we might recognize that we feel bad or upset, but it's hard to identify the emotion more specifically than that. Are you feeling frustrated or irritated or angry? Perhaps Marcella determines she is feeling discouraged, demoralized, or even hopeless.

At first, you might just want to practice noticing (and writing down) these three things—situation, thought, emotion—until they come more easily or naturally. You can note them in an app on your phone or on a piece of paper. Try to do it as close to the instance as possible. After you feel more comfortable identifying the thoughts, in particular, it's time to start thinking about how to respond to or revise those automatic thoughts.

Respond to Unhelpful Thoughts With Helpful Ones

This is the part at which you think of something you can tell yourself in response to, or perhaps instead of, the thought that you had. So, in the case of "it's no use," you might say, "I knew it wouldn't work out every time, and sometimes it seems like it *is* working" or, perhaps, "Maybe we got a few more people to vote in this election than might have voted otherwise." Maybe a mantra like "focus on the long game" would be helpful when experiencing losses or setbacks.

Marcella notices what effects these responses have on the reactions she was having. If the reactions are (still) unpleasant or are undesired emotions, she might evaluate the intensity of these emotions. Perhaps she still feels discouraged, but the feeling is a little less intense. Maybe she now feels like "hopeless" is too strong a word for how she feels about the situation. This outcome (still feeling unpleasant emotions but feeling them less strongly) may not feel all that compelling to you. Perhaps you are having automatic thoughts right now, such as: "Why even do this cognitive reappraisal thing if

I'm still going to feel discouraged at the end?" It's true. This technique does not eliminate all negative emotions from our lives, nor does any technique of which we are aware, and nor should any. To be honest, negative emotions are part of life, and they sometimes provide us with useful information. We can tolerate them. This is just a strategy for turning down the volume or intensity of negative emotions so that they don't get in our way as much.

Now go ahead and try this yourself. Think about a recent time when you were feeling something intensely or feeling a way you didn't want to feel. What was the situation? In other words, if someone asked you what happened, what would you say? Again, in everyday conversation, we tend to associate negative emotions with external stressors or situations. But, according to the theory behind cognitive therapy, the automatic thoughts in between lead to or at least exacerbate these unwanted emotions.

Once you've noted the situation, move on to whatever is easiest for you next. Sometimes it's easiest to identify the emotion. That's fine. And don't forget: Sometimes we have more than one emotion at a time—even seemingly contradictory ones! You could feel relieved and guilty at the same time, or excited and anxious, or even sad and happy. Try to be as specific as possible. If "bad" or "upset" is what comes to mind, see if you can answer the question "What kind of bad?" Did you feel frustrated? Disappointed? Mad? Identifying our emotions precisely will help us manage them the way we want to. If this is hard for you, try looking up a list of emotion words. You can Google "emotion words," and lists will come up. Some cognitive therapy apps have these built in, too, and you get to choose your emotion from a drop-down menu. You may also wish to look for an "emotion wheel" or "feelings wheel" online like the one we've provided in Figure 3.2. Look at the list and see which word or words seem to fit best. Some versions even include words that describe body sensations in addition to emotions.

FIGURE 3.2. The Feeling Wheel

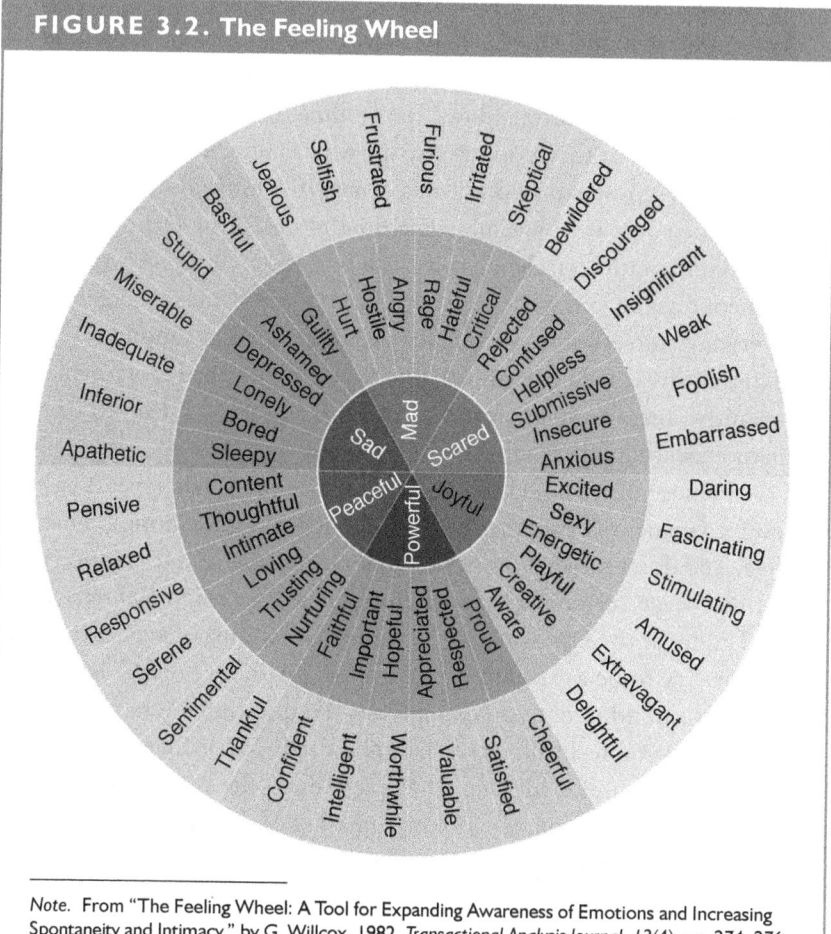

Note. From "The Feeling Wheel: A Tool for Expanding Awareness of Emotions and Increasing Spontaneity and Intimacy," by G. Willcox, 1982, *Transactional Analysis Journal, 12*(4), pp. 274–276 (https://doi.org/10.1177/036215378201200411). Copyright 1982 by Taylor & Francis. Adapted with permission.

Now let's discuss the automatic thoughts. Remember: Even if you're identifying these last, in real life they are believed to come before the negative emotion. Perhaps you're pretty aware of the automatic thought that led to that emotion. Maybe it's a sentence you tell yourself all day, every day. Maybe it's an image that pops into your head frequently, and you try to get rid of it as fast as you can. But maybe it's not all that easy for you to identify your automatic thoughts. Don't worry; most of us aren't aware of our automatic thoughts until we start to focus on them. You can learn to tune into them. Once you have identified a thought (or think you might have), write it down.

You might find it useful to make a diagram that looks like the one we presented earlier, only this time, fill in your own situation, thought(s), and emotions or other reactions:

situation → thought → emotion or reaction

Take a look at that diagram. Does it make sense? Does it make sense that a person in that situation, having that thought, would feel the way you did?

If you haven't already done so, now you can identify the emotion that (presumably) followed the automatic thought. Remember to be as specific as you can. Like so many things, this, too, will get easier with practice.

The first few times you do this, just stop there. You don't have to go through the whole process at first. It's good to get some practice just identifying your automatic thoughts.

The next part is probably the most powerful part of the process: You are going to generate a response to your automatic thought or a different response to the situation. What do we mean by that? Well, these responses can take multiple forms. They can take the form of what you'd like to say back to your automatic thought to encourage yourself to question it. Or they can be another way of looking at the situation—looking at it from another point of view.

Remember how, in the example, Marcella thought, "It's no use"? There were a few ways to respond to that (actually, there may be infinite ways to respond to any automatic thought; there's no "right" answer). One way is to question the automatic thought itself and look for evidence. Is it really "no use"? What is the evidence for that? What is the evidence against it? Perhaps more importantly: Does the thought make you feel better? Worse? Does it decrease your motivation to do the things that are important to you? Does it make you feel worse about people in your life? Those are the types of questions we ask to evaluate helpfulness.

Marcella might ask herself, "Is there evidence that it was of 'no use' to expend energy canvassing for my candidate?" If Marcella lives in a district that has always voted for one party, and she was canvassing for the candidate for the other party, and that candidate was likely to lose by at least 50 points, one could argue that it was no use.

Marcella could certainly question the definition of "no use": What would we call "useful" in this situation? What were the original goals? Looking at it this way, we can evaluate whether the "no use" thought is accurate. Obviously, winning is usually the most desired outcome in an election. But are there other positive outcomes that might happen, even if winning does not? Letting people know about the alternatives? Pushing the winning candidate to accommodate other voters in the district, even just a little bit?

Alternatively, it might make more sense to evaluate the thought in terms of its helpfulness. What are the consequences of that thought? What effect is it having? In addition to potential emotional consequences (feeling discouraged), are there practical or behavioral consequences? What if Marcella found herself withdrawing from not only her political activities but also from just about everything? Maybe she's not answering the phone or is staying in bed as long as possible in the morning and getting into bed as soon as possible when she gets home? If Marcella's reactions look like this, her thoughts may be causing her real trouble. (If you find you are having trouble getting out of bed or withdrawing from activities, or both, this might be a good time to seek help as described in Chapter 8.)

So how might you respond to negative thoughts, such as "It's no use"? If you're going the rational/irrational route, you might try to talk yourself out of it, so to speak—for example: "It's not totally useless. We are building a community and learning skills that might help us tackle other issues together" or "At least we're making some people think about these issues more."

In terms of helpfulness, the key is not to dismiss the thought or try to suppress it but to try not to dwell on it: "This particular effort might not work out, it's true. You win some, you lose some." You might work to replace the unhelpful thought with this new one. It won't happen immediately, but if you find yourself having the thought a lot and reminding yourself of the new way of framing the situation or perspective on it, your brain may learn to skip right to the new perspective (it's amazing!). You can also try to focus on something else, especially if the "it's no use" thought is often followed by "I don't know why I waste my time; this is totally hopeless. The whole world is a mess, and there's nothing I can do about it." You might try to shift your focus to something more rewarding. You might decide this is a time to step up your self-care to keep yourself afloat (see Chapter 8 for more on self-care).

Categorize Unhelpful Thoughts

There are several common kinds of unhelpful thoughts. You can find lists of these categories online (e.g., Stress & Development Lab, n.d.). You may find that once you start noticing your automatic thoughts more, you tend to rely pretty heavily on some types of these thoughts rather than others. For example, earlier, we alluded to a category called "should statements." Albert Ellis, who developed rational emotive therapy (now known as rational emotive behavior therapy), emphasized the importance of these "necessitist" thoughts and pointed out that it is often more helpful to conceptualize these notions as preferences rather than requirements or demands (Ellis, 1987). These are things we tell ourselves about standards that we would ideally be meeting and are not, ways in which we judge ourselves (or others!) for coming up short or being inadequate in some way. Examples include: "I shouldn't have done that," or "I shouldn't have to sit through this," or "I have to stop doing that!" (Notice that the word "should" doesn't necessarily appear in all of these statements. "Must" and "ought" can be culprits, too.) "Shoulds" can apply to other people, too: "He shouldn't be so needy." "They shouldn't talk so much."

When we tell ourselves that things should be otherwise, we are adding a layer of morality to something that might really be more of a wish. Questions to ask yourself in response to these thoughts might include: "Who says . . .?" ("Who says I should never forget anything?") or "Why?" ("Why shouldn't I have to sit through meetings? People have to sit through meetings all the time!") Often "shoulds" reflect a preference—a preference for things to be ideal, or perfect, or at least closer to those ideals. But it doesn't help matters to turn that preference into some kind of moral obligation that isn't being met. Indeed, Ellis contended that doing so may increase the probability of becoming depressed rather than just momentarily frustrated or disappointed.

We introduce other categories of negative thoughts elsewhere in the book. Some include catastrophizing (expecting the worst possible outcome), magnification (typically of something negative), and mind-reading (thinking you know what someone else is thinking—and it's typically about you and bad). You don't *have* to take the step of categorizing your automatic thoughts, but recognizing these patterns can help us develop helpful ways to respond that can become habit more readily.

PRACTICE

Now that you've walked through this process, think about how you might incorporate this reflection exercise into your daily life, so you can get more practice. With practice, the newer thoughts will come more easily, and in time, they will even replace the less helpful thoughts. This is about habit formation. You've spent your whole life forming the thought-habits you have now, so new habits will take time and practice.

How do you want to practice? At first, you might want to set an alarm on your phone to remind you to go through this activity at the end of the day (eventually, you'll want to do it in the moment when an unpleasant emotion arises). And then you will want to write down the situation, thought(s), and emotions. There is a worksheet for this process that you can find published in some other books or online (e.g., Vivyan, 2010). Or you can just keep a notebook with you and jot down your challenging situations, thoughts, and reactions there. Perhaps these days it's easier to keep a log digitally, even on your phone. As we mentioned, there are now apps that walk you through this process. We like MoodKit (see https://www.thriveport.com/products/moodkit/), but there are other good ones out there, too. Some apps are not so great: As one recent article we came across said, mental health apps are basically the Wild West—anyone can make one and sell it, and many are not vetted by mental health professionals. Read reviews before you pay for one (see the Appendix; we provide links to some review sites there), or try out a couple to see which one seems to match up with the process we outline here or to figure out which one you like the most. The point is to practice the techniques, so you want to make it as easy for yourself as possible to get regular practice into your day.

"When," you may wonder, "will I see the benefits of all this work?" Thought-habits are a lot like other habits: Change takes practice, and it takes time. You might find yourself feeling a bit better in the moment as you generate responses to your automatic thoughts. And over the longer term, you will likely find yourself catching those automatic thoughts more quickly, perhaps even responding to thoughts before they are complete. Eventually, perhaps the automatic thoughts will be replaced by more helpful ones. And then you will find you are a bit less emotionally reactive or at least that your emotional reactivity doesn't get in the way of your pursuing your goals as much. If you're not seeing the progress you were hoping for, that might be a time to seek out a therapist; we provide some resources for finding therapists in the appendix.

BOTTOM LINE

You may have been surprised to discover that an entire chapter of this book focuses on thoughts. We all experience stressors—they're a part of life—and social action and justice work certainly come with their share of stressors. Adjusting our lives to include social action and justice work can also bring stress. The thoughts we have about these stressors, even those thoughts we might not realize we're having, can impact the way we experience and react to the circumstances.

The good news is that we can learn new habits of thinking, which can help us to cope with the inevitable ups and downs of our work in ways that are more in line with our values and intentions. Changing our thought-habits can improve our quality of life and make us more effective at the work we are doing to make the world a better place. It takes time, and it requires specific effort. But it can be done.

CHAPTER 4

MANAGING EMOTIONS: OTHER APPROACHES

Marcella, whom we introduced in the previous chapter, loves her work at the nonprofit and finds it to be really meaningful. But some days, she feels like getting out of bed is a chore. Being at work is, well, work—not just because it requires focused attention but because it requires thinking about stressful and emotionally difficult topics. As we saw in Chapter 3, Marcella also engages in social justice work outside of her job, and this work can be frustrating and can require stamina. On top of all of those stressors, Marcella is the only Latina woman in her organization, and the vast majority of her colleagues are White. Marcella gets along well with her colleagues, but she often feels isolated—like she needs to carry a lot—on her own. Sometimes it's as though everything she says or does informs her colleagues' opinions of all people from Colombia, or even all Latinas, if they don't know many personally. The weight of that pressure takes a toll.

In Chapter 3, we discussed a common cognitive technique for managing emotions: cognitive reappraisal. In this chapter, we explore other approaches to uncomfortable emotions. We start with the concepts of acceptance and cognitive defusion as defined in acceptance and commitment therapy (ACT).

ACCEPTANCE

We probably all have a basic idea of what acceptance is. In ACT, *acceptance* is conceptualized as being the opposite of experiential avoidance. In other words, rather than trying to change or escape our thoughts or feelings, we accept them as they are, especially when trying to change or avoid them is causing problems for us.

To be clear, we are not asking you to accept external circumstances (this book is, after all, called *Being the Change*—not *Resigning Yourself to the World as It Is*). Yes, some things are beyond our control, and continuing to fight them may not be the best use of your resources. But here, we're talking about accepting your internal experiences: your thoughts and feelings. You might think of this as dropping the rope in the tug-of-war with your undesired feelings and actually standing with them face to face—just being present with them without trying to change what you are feeling.

Another situation in which acceptance can be helpful is if you find yourself having bothersome secondary and tertiary emotions. What are those? They're emotions *about* your emotions or emotions about the emotions you have about your emotions. Sound ridiculous? It's not. We all do it. Do you ever find you're more frustrated than you want to be? Wish that some things didn't affect you so much? That's what we mean. Judging our experiences of emotions can lead to more emotions.

Anxiety is one emotion that often leads to secondary and tertiary emotions. Perhaps once you notice your anxiety, you worry about it. That's secondary anxiety: anxiety about your anxiety. Or maybe when you find yourself running through the same cognitive reappraisal process over and over again with respect to anxiety-provoking thoughts, you get mad at yourself. That anger is secondary to the anxiety (some argue that anger is almost always a secondary emotion).

Acceptance helps with these. You might say it replaces them:

Instead of being anxious about my anxiety, I'm accepting my anxiety. Instead of being angry about my anxiety, I'm accepting my anxiety. I am anxious right now. There are times in my life when I am more anxious (or sad or angry) than other times. These feelings are part of the ebb and flow of life. Instead of trying to change the emotion, I am accepting that right now, I feel anxious.

Let's go back to an issue Luke is having (we introduced him in Chapter 1). He and his partner have decided it's the right time for them to buy a house. They have enough for a down payment and are looking at different houses in the area. As first-time home-buyers, they didn't understand just how difficult getting a house would be. While out looking at houses with his partner, Luke is finding that each experience leads to frustration, anxiety, and sometimes anger. They find plenty of houses they like, but as soon as they talk to their agent about putting in an offer, either they are the 14th offer or the house has already been sold. This cycle repeats itself time after time. Luke feels that "it shouldn't be like this"—that they should be able to buy a house more easily. One approach would, of course, be to question the "should" in those statements. Alternatively, Luke could work on accepting that this is a point of suffering without judging whether the situation should or should not be as it is.

Again, we want to remind you of an important distinction: Acceptance is not resignation; it's not giving up. We'll come back to that issue, but for the moment, just bear in mind that we are not asking you to give up, either on managing your emotions or on being the change you wish to see. We are just saying that our human experience involves experiencing numerous emotions. Acceptance of that reality is often helpful in moving past them.

The acceptance we're talking about here involves accepting that we do not have 100% control over our emotions. Some say we don't have *any* control over our emotions. But at a minimum, we can probably agree that, as humans, we do not have complete control over our feelings. It follows that we can try to accept that, as humans, we will sometimes feel anxiety even if we don't want to. Or maybe one can even try to accept that, "as a relatively anxious human, I might have more anxiety than most" or that "I'm in a situation right now that is anxiety provoking."

Thoughts like these might help us to acknowledge the anxiety and then move on in pursuit of our goals. That's the "commitment" part of ACT: staying committed to our goals. This is what we mean when we say acceptance is not resignation. We are not suggesting that, after experiencing race-related aggression, you need to just say, "Ah, well, there's racism in the world" and then ignore it. Definitely not.

A friend (and college chaplain) once told me (Dara) that some people find the word "acknowledge" to be more on point and more palatable than "accept." The friend discovered this in the context of a class she was teaching on grief. Students bristled at the notion of accepting the loss of someone close to them as though doing so meant saying the loss was okay when it felt the total opposite of okay. My friend clarified that the kind of acceptance they were going for was accepting that reality is reality rather than insisting that it should not be—not really saying that it is okay or acceptable in some way. So maybe acceptance is not the best word for you; feel free to use your own language. But there is an argument to be made that acknowledging the reality is actually a necessary first step in doing something about something unacceptable when there's something to be done. For example, if we don't acknowledge that women's voices are frequently silenced and we act as if all is well in the gender-relations world, we will likely not do much to make the situation better.

In the case of grief, there's not much we can do to make the situation or external reality better. Sometimes we need to grieve and feel pain. But perhaps letting go of the fight that the reality shouldn't be the reality can help us to do that emotional work. Obviously, this is easier said than done.

The notion, though, may apply to a number of irreconcilable situations. Let's return to the situation in which Marcella's candidate lost the election. While she knows she cannot change the election results, she can accept the loss and feelings that come with it and, at the same time (or perhaps a bit later!), focus on the societal and cultural forces that may have contributed to the loss and keep working on those. Perhaps your work is grant funded, and your organization did not get a grant it very much deserved. Can you refocus your energy on doing the work you are passionate about in other corners, in other, perhaps, smaller ways with fewer resources or on writing the next grant?

We are not trying to push this acceptance notion. We're just offering it up as an option, particularly if cognitive reappraisal does not seem like the way to go.

COGNITIVE DEFUSION

Like its sister concept, acceptance, cognitive defusion is a component of ACT. The theory behind ACT is complex and beyond the scope of this book. Fortunately, however, the Association for Contextual Behavioral Science has some great information and background online (see Hayes, n.d.). The overall goal of ACT is psychological flexibility, and one of the basic tenets is that our use of language, or the things we tell ourselves, may get in the way of that flexibility. *Cognitive defusion*—recognizing that you and your thought are separate entities—can help us unentangle ourselves from unhelpful words.

In Chapter 3, we talked about how we can adjust our thought-habits so that we have more helpful thinking patterns in our daily lives. Cognitive defusion takes a slightly different approach (although the end result may be similar in that it helps us to be less influenced by those unhelpful thoughts): ACT considers thoughts to be among the psychological phenomena that we actually can't control. At the same time, ACT reminds us that we are not our thoughts. We do not have to take them literally, we do not have to assume they are true, and we do not have to identify with them. This last bit is what cognitive defusion is all about: We are defusing ourselves from our thoughts.

Let's come back to Luke, who was drawn to a career in social work because of his desire to help people but didn't like the amount of time he was spending on paperwork. Luke might have thoughts such as, "This is such a waste of time" or "I am wasting my life." Certainly, the thought of wasting one's life would make most of us feel depressed and demoralized. And most of us, if we had that thought, might feel upset immediately without questioning the veracity of the thought.

Cognitive reappraisal offers us one way to examine such thoughts by looking for evidence for and against, considering whether the thought is helpful, and looking for other ways to evaluate the situation. ACT suggests, instead, that we distance ourselves from our thoughts or remind ourselves that our thoughts are not necessarily true. We might use such phrases as "I just had the thought that I'm wasting my life," or "That's just a thought" and "Just because I had that thought doesn't mean it's true."

This idea is more radical than it might seem. If left to our own devices, we tend to accept our thoughts as true. So, it's no wonder that thoughts such as, "I am so stupid," are damaging. It's helpful to stop and catch those.

If you're familiar with the categories of unhelpful thoughts in cognitive therapy, you might notice that both "I am so stupid" and "I'm wasting my life" are overgeneralizations. So why not remind yourself of that? You can, certainly. But sometimes people find that identifying the unhelpful thought doesn't help that much. Some people find that if they try cognitive reappraisal (and we really mean *try*—not just once but many times) and they find themselves feeling stuck, cognitive defusion can be an easier way to reduce the power of that thought. You might think of cognitive defusion as realizing that you normally see the world through goggles, taking them off, and putting them inches away from your face to really see and understand how thoughts shape and structure your world (and affect your behaviors).

It may also be helpful to try an exercise shared by Steven Hayes in the workbook *Get Out of Your Mind & Into Your Life* in which you take a word, such as "milk," and consider what milk is, what it feels like, and all of the other attributes of milk. Consider what it tastes like. What does sour milk taste like? Jot these ideas down on a piece of paper and then go to a quiet place where you can be undisturbed for a few minutes. When you are comfortable, say the word "milk" out loud and then repeat it as fast as you can for about 20 to 40 seconds. Be sure to time yourself because that time period is essential to establishing the point of this exercise. Say "milk" over and over again until the timer goes off. After you have done this, write down what happened to the meaning of the word. Did the word still bring up the image of milk that you had before the exercise? Did you notice anything new happen from doing this exercise?

For most of us, the meaning of the word begins to fall away while doing this exercise, and what is left is just the sounds and sensations. What we think of as "milk"—the liquid we put on our cereal—has faded away. Now, try something slightly different. Take a negative thought you have about yourself and put it into one word (shorter is better) and try this exercise with that. First, though, write down what that word means to you. Then, rate it for how distressing it is to think this word applies to you—from 0 (*not at all*) to 100 (*maximally distressing*) and how much the word *does* apply to you (from 0 to 100 again). Now take the word and do the same thing you did with "milk," saying it as fast as you can while still pronouncing it for the time period provided earlier. What was this like for you? Redo the ratings just described. How did your distress and belief levels change?

Considering the thought or word you used in the previous exercise, it may sometimes be helpful to think about why you might be having that thought in the first place, especially when it's really "sticky" and you don't seem to be making much headway with cognitive reappraisal. Perhaps it's something a parent said to you. Or perhaps it's something that might have been, in some ways, adaptive in the past but is not serving you well now. Sometimes when we recognize where the thought comes from, that can help us realize that it's not The Truth (note the capital *T*s). Separating ourselves from our thoughts can help us to accept that we have the thoughts we have without letting them take over.

MINDFULNESS

One practice that can help us defuse from our thoughts is mindfulness. You may have a regular mindfulness practice, or perhaps you've tried it but not stuck with it, or maybe you haven't really felt like you had the time or the inclination to try it. Mindfulness is one of those concepts that became wildly popular rather quickly in the United States (despite having been around globally for quite some time), and when concepts become widespread like that, they often also start to drift a little from what they were originally about.

Mindfulness, in the Buddhist tradition, involves awareness of the past, present, and future and focus on both self and others. In addition, it has components of flexibility, skillfulness, purposefulness, wisdom, and ethics. In contemporary Western psychology, mindfulness is often described as nonjudgmental awareness of the present moment. It often involves acceptance of emotional states and is used as a self-regulation or coping strategy. In the late 1970s and early 1980s, two major figures in clinical psychology incorporated mindfulness into their treatments—Jon Kabat-Zinn, who established mindfulness-based stress reduction (MBSR) at the University of Massachusetts Chan Medical School (UMMS), and Marsha Linehan, the founder of dialectical behavior therapy at the University of Washington. I (Jamie) went through the program at UMMS during my fellowship there and got firsthand experience with the program.

In Kabat-Zinn's (2005) book, *Full Catastrophe Living*, he discusses seven attitudinal factors that are the pillars of a mindfulness practice. Each is cultivated as you practice mindfulness. They are interconnected. *Nonjudging* is the first pillar and is about the judgment we place on our experiences. We are constantly judging and reacting to the inner and outer experiences, and mindfulness gives us the opportunity to step out of these processes. This benefit becomes more noticeable as we practice mindfulness.

Another pillar, *beginner's mind*, is about being able to see things in our lives—people, places, experiences, or objects—as if we are seeing them for the first time. I (Jamie) use the example of an infant trying a new food for the first time and what that experience is like. For adults, it's about trying to shed our preconceived notions and expectations to see things as if we have never seen them before. This is especially useful in our closest relationships because we often have a narrative in our head as we interact with our partner, spouse, mother, child, or close friend. For example, we might think, "Here it comes. I know what he's going to say." Instead, try to see them as they are, without our past experiences clouding our judgment, can be useful in really hearing them and in their feeling heard. This experience can be quite transformative.

Another pillar is *nonstriving*, which is essentially nondoing. This can be challenging for people who feel that they always need to be on the go and actively doing things. Nonstriving is not necessarily about not doing anything in your life; it's about mindfulness itself and not striving for any particular goal while practicing. Indeed, when entering an MBSR program, the instructor will ask you to write down your goals for starting the mindfulness program. After you write them down, they purposefully tell you that you will not be working on them. You will be working on simply paying attention to whatever is unfolding at the time and not trying to "change" the experience—simply observing. In mindfulness, there is no goal to reach or objective to meet.

Acceptance, discussed earlier, is another of Kabat-Zinn's pillars and is defined as a willingness to see things as they are. It's about not fighting the experience or feeling that you are having, even if it is unpleasant. Even if you are not satisfied with your life, self, or experience, you accept those realities. Does that mean you can't change, or can't work for change, or even want something different? Absolutely not. However, you can do those things and simultaneously be willing to see things as they are. Take each moment as it comes and be open and accepting of the feeling, thought, or experience you are having without trying to change it or impose your own ideas or expectations onto it. It's often the struggle we have with our negative emotions or thoughts—and not the actual emotion or thought—that cause us distress. If we can just make room for these emotions and thoughts and accept that they are there, we may find our energy is freed up to work on other important things in our life.

The last pillar we want to discuss here is *letting go*. As you begin your practice of mindfulness, you will start to find you are more likely to hold on to certain thoughts. Your mind may keep coming back to specific thoughts or feelings over and over again. It may be hard to let them go. You may also find that there are some things you *want* to hold on to and go over again and again because they are pleasant thoughts, memories, or feelings. In a similar vein, there may be things that you want to avoid thinking about or experiencing because they are too painful, and therefore, you may not allow these thoughts into your experience. This is why the pillar of letting go is so important: It is about just observing what is happening, moment by moment, and not trying to manipulate our experience in any way.

Mindfulness can be practiced through meditation or yoga, and it can also be a way of approaching daily activities, such as eating and walking. Exercises for practicing meditation are abundant. The key to mindfulness practice is engaging with your breath or senses to bring yourself to the present moment. The first and easiest type of meditation is a mindful breathing exercise. It is about focusing your attention on your breath. Why start with your breath? People new to mindfulness practice are learning to pay attention on purpose and in a particular way to each moment. One of the easiest ways to connect to the present moment is to pay attention to your breathing. We are always breathing. It's automatic and is a good anchor to the moment. While this is one of many types of meditations, it's a great beginners exercise. In the appendix, you'll find some great resources—including apps—to try.

Through mindfulness practice, you may become more aware of your own reactions. You may find it easier to let go of undesired emotions rather than latch on to them. Some of these outcomes relate to concepts in Buddhism. They don't typically just happen because you intend for them to, though; they take practice. This is where the meditation practice comes in. Also, of course, people report finding the practice relaxing and may find that it helps them cope with stress. The benefits can be many. If you're already practicing—awesome. If you aren't, you may want to give it a(nother) try and see if you notice any benefits. It doesn't have to be hours a day, but the more regularly you practice, the more you may feel the benefits.

While we are suggesting mindfulness in this section as a tool and strategy to improve quality of life and emotional stability, we need to mention that being mindful can also have direct benefits to our social action work. Sharon Salzberg, in the book *Real Change: Mindfulness to Heal Ourselves and the World*, discusses the role that mindfulness can bring to our lives in how we interact with our thoughts and with suffering. Unfortunately, when suffering is what pulls us to this work, it can also take a toll on our mental health. Recognizing through mindfulness that our negative thoughts regarding situations or others' suffering is only "visiting" and doesn't have to be our storyline or experience can help us be able to move forward through the pain to take the action we need to make a difference in the world.

GRATITUDE

Take a few moments to think about the first time you learned about gratitude. Perhaps your parents made you write thank-you notes to relatives and friends for gifts you received. It may be that learning your manners, such as using "please" and "thank you" was the first time you expressed gratitude verbally. If you are part of a faith community, perhaps it is something that you express during services or prayers. Some people worry that it feels selfish to practice gratitude for what you have, especially if you work with people who have less. But as it turns out, gratitude can be a wonderful antidote to negative emotions. One way to think about this might be to think of the practice of *gratitude* as "balancing out" the brain's tendency to focus on the negative.[1] Practicing gratitude forces you to spend

---

[1]For more on this tendency, see the book *Why Buddhism Is True* (Wright, 2018), listed in the Appendix.

at least a little time and energy looking for the positives, and, over time, it becomes a habit.

What does it mean to practice gratitude? This kind of practice can take many forms. Some people keep a gratitude journal, and every night before bed, they jot down a few things they are grateful for. Some of us might benefit from creating some kind of cue or reminder of the many wonderful things in our lives—for example, making a collage of photos of loved ones and hanging it over your desk. Gratitude can also be more explicit in terms of expressing appreciation for coworkers or others in your community. (And guess what? This type of gratitude has benefits for the other person, too!) Along these same lines, gratitude can be expressed at any time. You don't have to wait to say thank you after someone does something nice for you. Consider sending your friends or loved ones a short note letting them know you are grateful for them, saying what you appreciate about them.

Importantly, we are not asking you to ignore frustrations or other negative emotions or experiences—we are not asking that you put on rose-colored glasses. Ideally, what we'd like to do is both be aware of the negative emotions or experiences and recognize the positives, too. Let's say that you work at an organization that helps those without stable housing. You might leave work thinking that the world is a cruel and unfeeling place and feeling frustrated by the many aspects of our society that make it extremely hard to get out of poverty. How might you practice gratitude in this case? Perhaps you might think of the folks you know who have had positive outcomes: clients you've worked with who do have stable housing now and maybe a job. You could orient toward a feeling of gratitude that your organization even exists or for your dedicated, compassionate colleagues. Obviously, these things don't make the harsh realities go away or even make them (much) less harsh. But they might help you stay afloat.

SOCIAL SUPPORT

Having a group of friends, family, or neighbors who provide support to you is a critical part of being the change. What does social support look like, and why is it important? *Social support* can be a person who just listens. Perhaps you are drained from your week, trying to place a refugee family in an apartment while the threat of deportation is looming. Having people you can talk to about your week, your emotions, and your experience can help alleviate the burden that is on your shoulders. How many times have thoughts run through your mind about a situation or experience that bothers you? You may never verbalize the issue (share it with another person) or get the opportunity to truly process it. Having a friend or someone to call and chat about the situation, even if that friend only provides empathy and has no concrete advice to give, can help you to cope and help decrease the stress that ensues. Don't underestimate the power of being validated or the benefits of talking through your feelings.

In addition to helping with the emotional aspect of your work, social support can also provide more tangible help. It can be the neighbor who walks your dog for you on the nights you work late. Or maybe your parents watch your kids so that you can organize a benefit. Both of these types of support help alleviate stress.

A lot of research supports the effect that social support has on decreasing stress levels and increasing one's quality and even length of life. Social support can help us manage difficult emotions and provide opportunities to experience some positive ones, too. Perhaps your desire to make these social connections is what attracted you to do the social action work you do. Often we meet amazing, like-minded folks through this work. However, it is important to maintain or develop relationships with people who are outside of that circle, too. Having a good laugh with a friend or sharing a meal with a neighbor is a good way to take a break from your work, connect with others, and reflect on life. Every time I (Jamie) take a night to go out with neighbors or friends, I find my battery gets recharged, and I can then come back to work with a greater level of vigor. What can you do to get this support and feel reenergized?

Take a few minutes and think of some people with whom you are close or people you would like to get to know better. Keep in mind that these individuals do not have to be colleagues from your work or anyone who is a part of your community group. Indeed, it's often more helpful to have a diverse group of friends who play different roles in your life. When was the last time you spent time with these people? Have there been opportunities to go out with them that you turned down? Could you find space in your schedule to spend time with someone who listens and is good company? While we agree that chatting with some of our support system via text or other sort of messaging can help and gives us an outlet, it can be helpful to have face-to-face contact with others, when possible. If you find that you have a lot of group texts with your neighbors, suggest that they come over one night to play cards or just to hang out on your porch. We're pretty confident that, most of the time, these occasions will provide a mood boost. And guess what: It turns out that providing social support is important, too. When you host your friends, you have the opportunity to talk to them, and you're also doing them a favor by giving them that social outlet. Remember this when you have the chance to be on the receiving end: Sometimes we are reluctant to take someone up on an offer to help or to talk, but they probably benefit from helping you out, too. Social support strengthens social bonds.

BEHAVIORAL EXPERIMENTS

Most of us probably have, at times, experienced boosts in positive emotions from at least some aspects of our social justice work. If you don't (at all), it might be important to think about whether you're participating in the activities that are most meaningful to you or whether you're participating in the ways that nourish you the most. But if you have found that organizing an event for a cause that you care about or working on a campaign for a candidate or an issue brings you energy and satisfaction (again, not at every single moment, but at times), that's great. If those moments seem to be less frequent over time, though, you may need to reach further back to remind yourself of how good they feel. Perhaps look at pictures from prior events or reread an email you got about your work on a grant or a newspaper article about the work that you do. And then, even if you don't feel like you have the energy, consider engaging in a similar activity.

Behavioral experiments ask that we test things out to see how they work. Not sure how something will make you feel? Do it and find out. Make sure you notice how you're feeling before, during, and after the behavior or activity. You can log your mood systematically (rate it from 0 to 10 in a notebook or on your phone at those three time points). The 0 and 10 will depend on what emotion you're rating. If it's anxiety you want to rate, 0 would be *absolutely no anxiety* and 10 would be *the most anxiety I've ever felt* (possibly a panic attack). You may want to rate more than one thing (i.e., happiness, accomplishment, contentment) before and after the activity. Alternatively, you could rate overall mood with 0 being *the worst I've ever felt* and 10 being *the best I've ever felt*. Cognitive behavior therapy suggests that we rate the amount of pleasure and our feelings of mastery. Some activities are energizing because they give us a feeling of accomplishment, not just because they are fun to do. Do what works for you, but documenting these feelings is important.

And then, the next time, don't forget to think back to how you felt rather than just go on how you *think* you will feel. Confused yet? The thing is this: You'd think we'd be good at figuring out what will make us feel better because, after all, we've been doing things for our whole lives. Lots of people think they would *hate* administrative work, for example, because they are really "people" people and they don't like desk work. These are things we think we know about ourselves.

But if we give it a try and notice how we feel afterward, we may be surprised. For example, a couple of years ago, I (Dara) went to canvass in a neighboring state for a weekend. I was not looking forward to it. I had been away at a conference the weekend before and missed time with my kids. I didn't know anyone else who was going and had volunteered to drive (4 hours) with a complete stranger or two or three. As it turned out, I had a great time. The woman who carpooled with me was so interesting and so much a kindred spirit that we got to know each other really well over that weekend (8 hours in a car will do that!). So that, in and of itself, was enormously rewarding and energizing. The canvassing itself was not bad, either. I got in a lot of steps doing something more meaningful than the treadmill. I spoke with some like-minded folks who were grateful for the work I was doing. And I got to meet the candidate.

Do you always meet the candidate? No. Does the candidate always win? No. But if you can notice the other aspects of the process that you find rewarding and remind yourself that you tend to find these things rewarding, you might just find you're making more effective choices about managing your emotion and motivation.

SPECIFIC EMOTIONS: ANGER, GUILT, AND SHAME

Some emotions are more challenging to deal with than others. Of course, different people find different emotions to be more or less challenging. But many people engaged in justice work report struggling with three in particular: anger, guilt, and shame.

Anger

For many of us, the decision to get more involved in justice work comes from strong feelings about one or more social problems or situations. Gloria Steinem said, "The truth will set you free, but first it will piss you off" (and, indeed, she has written a book with that title; see Steinem, 2019). So maybe anger isn't all bad. Audre Lorde wrote about the role of anger in working toward justice, including in her essay "The Uses of Anger: Women Responding to Racism," in which she said, "Anger expressed and translated into action in the service of our vision and our future is a liberating and strengthening act of clarification" (Lorde, 2020, p. 57).

But how do we get from angry to free, liberated, and strong?

Each of us has our own history with strong feelings, including anger, that shapes how comfortable we are with those emotions, how we respond to them, and how we feel about feeling them. This last category—how we feel about feeling them—involves what are called "secondary emotions" or "meta-emotions."

Some posit that anger itself is almost always a *secondary emotion*—a feeling about a feeling. Perhaps hurt underlies the anger; we feel angry that someone made us feel hurt. Anger is, of course, complex. It can come from a feeling that things are not the way they *should* be in response to injustice or unfairness. It can come from feeling threatened.

Some of us are more comfortable with anger than others. Some of us recognize anger as very familiar, perhaps because we grew up in situations in which our rights were not respected or in which we or our loved ones were mistreated on a regular basis. Others of us may find anger to be fairly new or foreign.

Many psychotherapists believe there is an important role for modeling how to understand and react to anger. How did your parents manage anger? What were the ways in which it was expressed?

Was anger something to avoid or fear? Was it a natural part of life, accepted alongside other emotions, whether positive or negative? The way anger was handled in our early life experiences may shape the way we feel about and respond to anger.

Anger can also be thought of as either constructive or destructive. Kristen Neff, in her book *Fierce Self-Compassion*, noted that much justice work comes out of constructive anger. Neff explained that constructive anger focuses on protection from harm and other wrongs and also focuses on justice without focusing the anger or blame on the person or persons responsible for that wrong.[2] This kind of anger can facilitate our trying to understand the processes that contribute to the harm and can direct our actions to create a more just world. Destructive anger, on the other hand, tends to focus on blaming people in a personal, hostile, and aggressive way. It can lead to defensiveness that interferes with our ability to think clearly. As we mentioned earlier, anger is often related to a strong feeling that things are not the way they *should* be. As a result, one way to approach anger is to catch those "should" thoughts that we talked about in Chapter 3.

Of course, you may well be right that things are not the way they ought to be. That's pretty much inherent in the concept of injustice! So, you may not want to talk yourself out of that thought with respect to its accuracy, but you may want to shift your focus a bit— perhaps from fixating on hostility toward those who are responsible to acknowledging that things are the way they are and then figuring

---

[2]Please do not take this distinction to mean that we will not hold others accountable or responsible for harms they may be perpetuating. Rather, we hope we can find ways to do just that while not expending too much of our own emotional energy on hostile blame. For more about the nuances in the way focusing on blame can be destructive, see Neff's (2021) *Fierce Self-Compassion* (listed in the Appendix) or the research she cites on this topic.

out what you and others (perhaps including those who are responsible!) can do about it. This process might fall under the acceptance and commitment heading: Accept (acknowledge) the way things are and commit to making the change. You're not avoiding the "should" thoughts; rather, you're noticing them, perhaps noticing the emotions they evoke, and then gently redirecting your attention (and perhaps the energy that often accompanies anger) to any actions you can take.[3]

This process is obviously not the only way to make use of feelings of anger in justice work, and it is not easy. But it may be helpful to remember that anger is not something we need to suppress or ignore. Indeed, it can be transformative.

Guilt

Guilt refers to personal, subjective, troubling feelings of having done something wrong to another person. You probably have an intuitive sense that doing things out of guilt is not ideal. And yet, perhaps some of our involvement in good causes is motivated in part by guilt: guilt about having survived, having privilege, having been complacent. Guilt is one of those emotions that may play an important role in society: It keeps us adhering to some moral rules. If we could just steal things from others, for example, without feeling any guilt, we might do it all the time.

However, if the justice work you do is mainly motivated by guilt, you may well burn out sooner. Again, we are not saying there's

---

[3]Another scheme for categorizing types of anger actually has a category named after Audre Lorde, mentioned earlier in this chapter. Myisha Cherry, a philosophy scholar at the University of California, Riverside, defined *Lordean rage* as anger directed at those who perpetuate racism that is transformed into necessary action (Cherry, 2021).

no reason to feel guilty (although certainly we do sometimes feel excessive guilt or take responsibility for things that are not our responsibility). We are just suggesting shifting the focus, redirecting to other sources of motivation.

One such other source of motivation is love. Civil rights activist and organizer Heather Booth reminds us to keep "love at the center": love for people, love for the work, and love for ourselves (Wasik, 2018, last para.). We are not suggesting that love and kindness will solve everything. As Austin Channing Brown noted in *I'm Still Here: Black Dignity in a World Made for Whiteness,* love that overemphasizes "niceness," that evades responsibility, and that waits for change (rather than working for it) does not help. Rather, she argued, we need love that is "troubled by injustice" (Brown, 2018, p. 176).

The author and feminist bell hooks took this idea further: "There can be no love without justice" (hooks, 2018, ebook location 7.0233). Booth, in a training I (Dara) attended, also, among her pleas for love, encouraged us to "hate injustice." We assume that most, if not all, of us reading this book are deeply troubled by injustice—as we are—and we think we should continue to be troubled by it; we are not suggesting otherwise. Rather, we are suggesting that shifting our internal focus in the direction of feelings like love might be more helpful to us in sustaining our justice work rather than acting out of feelings of guilt.

Love for people, as Booth put it, may relate to empathy. When we experience love for others, we open ourselves up to feel their pain and struggles. It may even explain why people who engage in justice work may, as a whole, score pretty high on empathy: We can't just sit with that pain; we feel compelled to do something about it. It leaves us uncomfortable and may even lead to guilt for the pleasures or ease in which we live our own lives. What if we tried to refocus on the love piece of the empathy rather than the guilt part? How might that impact our experience of the work we are doing and our energy for it?

Guilt might also be associated with particular thoughts, of course, such as, "I'm not doing enough" or "I shouldn't have let this happen." Remember that you can also use cognitive reappraisal here. What would be "enough"? Are you single-handedly (or even not-single-handedly) responsible for others' suffering? Perhaps it's more helpful to think of ourselves as responsible for working toward solutions rather than being responsible for others' suffering.

Guilt can be a barrier in other ways, too. Perhaps you feel guilty taking time away from your partner or family to do more social justice work, even if, ultimately, that work aligns with values you and your partner share or is work that will make the world a better place for your children. Notice these feelings and think about how you want to respond to them. Don't assume that because you feel guilty means that you should skip the event or activity. Remember: Just because you think or feel it doesn't mean it's true.

Heather Booth's reminder to keep love at the center mentions love for self. Sacrificing everything (including your well-being) for the greater good probably is not the way to go. If you've ever taken a commercial airplane flight, you're probably familiar with the instructions you get about fastening your own oxygen mask before attending to someone who needs help. The same is true here. You won't be of much use to any cause if you burn out. We talk more about self-compassion in Chapter 8.

Given these realities, if you are contemplating engaging in an activity that doesn't seem meaningful to you, that you are dreading, and that you find draining because you find yourself thinking, "But I should . . ."—and these thoughts are accompanied by feelings of guilt—maybe you "shouldn't." Maybe you can refocus your energy in a direction that feels more in line with love and with your values. And be sure your move in that direction is not motivated as much by guilt.

Shame

> *Do the best you can until you know better. Then when you know better, do better.*
> —Maya Angelou (Harper's Bazaar Staff, 2017, para. 8)

Shame is the self-focused emotion associated with having behaved in a way that is inconsistent with one's values.[4] Shame does not seem like a feeling that needs to be inherently involved in our work to make the world a better place. Yet many of us have struggled with it, particularly as we may be gaining more insight into the ways that we perpetuate harmful systems, such as White supremacy. We now know that all humans have implicit biases. It follows that we all commit microaggressions whether we know it or not. And when we become aware of these behaviors that may have offended our colleagues or members of the communities in which we live and work, we may feel terrible.

So, what to do? Perhaps a coworker or a neighbor points out that you said something that reflects your privilege. Or maybe you used the wrong pronouns when addressing a coworker, referring to her or them as "him." Perhaps you felt your heart rate accelerate or your face got hot; perhaps you said something defensive, without really thinking. Reflecting back on it, you may start to feel these same physiological and emotional manifestations of shame. You know you should start thinking about how to repair the situation, but the intense arousal that accompanies thinking about the harm you may have caused makes it hard for you to think straight.

Step 1, then, is probably to try to reduce that arousal, to get to a place where you *can* think straight so that you can respond

---

[4]It is this focus on the self that differentiates shame from guilt, according to some researchers. Guilt focuses on the regretted behavior, whereas shame focuses on more global self-condemnation as a result of that behavior.

intentionally. Note that you don't have to "get it right" in the moment, necessarily—and, indeed, it may be impossible for you to do so. In many cases, we have the opportunity to return to the situation later and say what we mean to say.

How to reduce the arousal? There are some good tips in this book in Chapter 6 and in the appendix. You may want to try an abdominal breathing exercise or a mindfulness exercise. You may want to do a self-compassion meditation or go for a walk in nature. You could use cognitive reappraisal. Check your thoughts and self-talk. You might catch yourself saying things you would never say to someone else. "Oh my god, I'm racist," for example. "I can't believe I said that. I am what's wrong with our society." Would you tell a well-meaning colleague they were racist or that they were the problem? Probably not. Perhaps you understand intellectually that our brains use biases as "shortcuts" and that our biases are the product of both our neurobiology and our life experience or upbringing, but, in the moment, you're pretty convinced you are a terrible human being. Notice those discrepancies. See if you can remind yourself that what you are is, in fact, a human being—probably not a terrible one. You are working on these things.

It may also help to talk to someone else you know who shares your concern about these issues. Chances are, they will have some stories like yours: times when they said or did things that they realized afterward may have caused harm. They may have ideas for you as to how best to move forward, or perhaps hearing their own stories will be validating, reminding you that your mistakes are human and that making mistakes like these is, unfortunately, inevitable, in this work.

Once you feel calmer, figure out how you can attempt to repair whatever harm might have occurred. It might involve bringing up the potential microaggression with the person or people you may have harmed. This can be stressful, too. Maybe your like-minded friend can also help you with this part. Script out what you want to say in advance, even if you won't read it verbatim. It can be helpful to plan out your words so you can be faithful to your own values and intentions as you move forward.

Let's come back to the pressure Marcella feels at "representing" all Colombian women or all Latinas at her workplace. How could she address this particular source of stress? Before we answer that, we want to emphasize that, of course, this should not be Marcella's problem to solve. Ideally, others in her organization are aware that this might be a source of stress for Marcella and are doing all they can to mitigate it, perhaps conducting thorough outreach, as they hire new employees, to recruit a more diverse staff and by being on the lookout for behaviors and norms that might center the White experience, and then working to change those behaviors and norms, among other strategies.

But as for Marcella's own coping with the situation? Well, she has options. She could, using cognitive reappraisal, remind herself that she is not responsible for representing any of the groups to which she belongs to her colleagues, even if she feels she might be. She could practice mindfulness, focusing perhaps on letting go of the stressful thoughts she has related to being "the only one like her" in her organization. This more detached approach may help her to see clearly what aspects of her work situation led to her feeling these pressures in the event that she wants to bring them up with her coworkers, and it may help her identify where the stress is coming from.

She might also join a group, either online or in her community, for professional women of color in majority White organizations. There, she might find she is not alone in this situation. Or perhaps she might find comfort in spending more time with family or other members of her community who share her background and don't put the same pressures on her that her White colleagues do. Again, we don't think Marcella should have to exert this much effort to deal with this unjust situation. But, while things are (hopefully) changing, there are things she can do to help keep herself afloat.

BOTTOM LINE

We will certainly come back to the topic of responding to different emotions throughout the course of this book (including in Chapter 8 on self-care). Experiencing a range of emotions is part of the human condition, as is the fact that some feel easier to manage than others. What's generally found to be helpful is having a variety of coping strategies, or ways of responding to emotions, and we hope that you have picked up some new strategies or approaches in this chapter and in Chapter 3. There also may be a time when you might benefit from psychotherapy to help you deal with your emotions, as we discuss later in Chapter 8.

We encourage you to be open-minded, to see what works and what doesn't. Remember that the goal is to keep these things from getting in the way of your living a life that is as consistent as possible with your own goals and values.

CHAPTER 5

INTENTIONAL COMMUNICATION

We all know how to communicate; we've been doing it our whole lives. But might we be able to do it more effectively? Everyone experiences misunderstandings, whether from the point of view of the person who's trying to communicate something or as the person who's trying to understand. And if you think back, some of these misunderstandings may have been hurtful or they may have led to a lot of time spent on something unnecessary—something that could have been clear from the start had the message been conveyed more effectively.

It may also be the case that the communication you are required to do in your change work is different from what you are used to. Consider a young person who is asked to go knock on doors in a community to get signatures for a petition. This can be a very intimidating experience, even for the most seasoned petition walkers. You don't know how the person coming to the door may respond or may feel about the issue you are canvassing for. What if they get combative or want to start an argument? How do you handle it? For someone young with little experience asking people for things, this situation might lead to anxiety. Communication skills can be helpful.

It's helpful to review communication skills even if you are a great communicator. For one thing, some of us have good communication skills, but we lack confidence in them. Here, practice can help. And for most of us, there is probably room to be even more intentional about how we're communicating, so reflecting on this subject is worthwhile.

Our social action work may put us in novel social situations in which we are less skilled or less confident. In addition to knocking on strangers' doors, perhaps you are asked to speak at a rally or to call potential donors to ask for money: These might be things you are not used to doing. You may find yourself having to advocate for a child or family in court or dealing with a situation of domestic violence in which you need to communicate effectively in an emotional situation. Or you might need to communicate with people much older or younger than you or across other cultural boundaries. And to be honest, even in more familiar contexts, interpersonal conflict can be a major source of stress, and sometimes improved communication skills can help.

Marsha Linehan, the founder of dialectical behavior therapy, referred to *interpersonal effectiveness* as the ability to communicate in ways that help you approach your own goals without alienating others or losing respect for yourself (Linehan, 2014). In other words, you want to communicate in ways that advance your goals, show respect for the people you are communicating with, and show respect for yourself. These seem to us like pretty desirable outcomes in a lot of situations.

COMMUNICATION STYLES

There are four main communication styles: (a) assertive, (b) passive, (c) passive-aggressive, and (d) aggressive. Assertive communication is highly valued in mainstream U.S. society—and, indeed, it has been shown to be effective in a lot of contexts, although that doesn't mean it's always the best. *Assertive communication* refers to expressing your thoughts in a direct and straightforward way. Sometimes assertive communication is characterized as acknowledging that both the speaker and the listener have needs and rights. (Aggressive communication, on the other hand, ignores the other person's rights.) Acknowledging both parties' rights seems consistent with Linehan's aforementioned definition of "interpersonal effectiveness"—not alienating the other person or losing respect for yourself.

Some of us tend to hedge a little when we talk and could probably stand to express ourselves more directly. For example, look at that last sentence! What words suggest "hedging"? "Tend"? "Probably"? Even "could . . . stand to" is a little indirect. How might we rewrite this sentence? Maybe this: "Many of us [it's probably more than some!] use tentative language and would benefit from speaking more directly to show more respect for our own ideas." There's nothing offensive about that wording; it's perfectly benign and, at the same time, more direct than the first version.

Of course, part of the reason for the hedging is that we are trying to be polite. Think for a moment about how we teach kids to ask for what they want. Early on in their verbal development, we get very excited when they say, "Want cookie" because it's preferable to (and clearer than) screaming. But soon after, the child who says, "I want a cookie!" is taught to say, "May I please have a cookie?"— asking instead of telling and asking politely, at that.

At this point, you may be thinking about the roles that culture and gender play in communication. These are important factors in communication, and so is status. So, when a White male physician says, "You need to exercise more," it may be better received than when a woman of color[1] who is a social worker says exactly the same words to the same person. In this situation, she might opt

---

[1]Some readers may prefer the term *BIPOC*—Black, Indigenous, (and) People of Color—which highlights the particular harms done to Black and Indigenous people in the United States. In this text, we use "woman (or person) of color," which is consistent with guidelines of the American Psychological Association, because several of our case examples identify in ways not explicitly named in the term "BIPOC."

for, "Have you thought about how you could get more exercise?" On the one hand, for the person speaking, moderating her speech in this way might feel like a burden, or she might feel irritated for further entrenching social inequities rather than actively reversing them. On the other hand, using a question instead of a statement might also feel like the practical thing to do and even the right, caring thing to do in her situation. We want to think about how directly we're expressing ourselves and be intentional about it based on our desired outcomes. Perhaps your goal is to have women of color in the health professions be taken more seriously. In that case, if you are in the social worker's place, you might prefer the more direct wording. But perhaps your goal is to preserve the therapeutic relationship with the patient. In this instance, you might choose the less direct wording. Linehan talks more about various goals in her writing on interpersonal effectiveness.

Passive responding typically involves putting the other person's needs first and perhaps even denying your own. Maybe you find that, in meetings, you are hesitant to speak at all. Perhaps you generally don't speak. And that's fine. But do you leave meetings upset because you feel like you had some really good ideas that either didn't get expressed or got expressed and then were dismissed? Think about how they were worded (if you or someone else shared them). Did you say, "I'm sure you're right, but I had this random idea that maybe we could do it this other way . . ."? Notice how that puts the other person on a higher plane than the person with the "random" idea. How else might you say it? Take a moment and jot down a rewording that might be more assertive.

What about just: "I'd like to propose that we consider _____." Does that wording make you cringe because of its directness? Are you thinking, "Ha! Yeah, except I would never say that. . . ." Well, might there be some space in between that kind of direct communication and what you are doing now? Could you make a stepwise plan to gradually get more and more direct, over time? For example, consider these different phrasings:

- "I'm sure you're right, but I had this random idea . . ."
- "I really appreciate all the ideas that have come up. I thought I might just add one . . ."
- "Related to what Sue said, I think we could . . ."
- "What about _____?"
- "I'd like to propose that we consider _____."
- "I think we should consider _____."
- "I disagree with what has been said for _____ reasons and think we should look at a different avenue. For instance, . . ."

Do any of those ideas sound comfortable? Remember: As you move toward more assertive self-expression—if you choose to—it will get more comfortable. And there's a bonus: Other people in your organization might feel empowered by your example, and perhaps they will express their thoughts more assertively (or *more*, period!) as a result. If you are a woman or a person of color, especially, you may be paving the way for others in your group. We talk more about the power of modeling in Chapter 7.

One barrier that individuals can encounter when working on assertiveness is social anxiety. Some of us tend not to speak out or speak up not because of lack of skill but, rather, because of anxiety about doing so. Some social anxiety is normal. Remember that with a moderate level of anxiety, we can perform well; however, when the anxiety becomes too high it can affect performance and lead to high levels of distress. If you feel that anxiety around social situations and engagement with others is having a major effect on your life (e.g., relationships, work, school, family), you may have a diagnosable and treatable condition called "social anxiety disorder" or "social phobia."

Did you know that social anxiety disorder is the most common anxiety disorder? Millions of Americans and individuals around the globe suffer with this disorder. Avoidance of social activities that involve speaking, eating, or writing in front of others, or experiencing extreme anxiety or distress when in these situations can be signs that you have this disorder. Perhaps you have spent your entire career or life avoiding public speaking or being in situations in which you either have to meet new people or be the center of attention. If this sounds like you, very effective evidence-based treatments are available that could help you work through this fear and make your social action work even more impactful!

Next, let's talk about passive-aggressive and aggressive communication.

We probably have more experience with these types of communication than we might like. Thoughts that are communicated in these ways (or *not* communicated in these ways) would often be more effectively expressed assertively. So, these might be good categories to listen for in your own speech, to try to think about how you might communicate a bit more directly, with respect for both your and the other person's ideas and needs. Some of these might come up more with family than with coworkers or other members of an organization, but they might come up in these settings, too.

Passive-aggressive communication appears, on the surface, to be passive: It's communication in which the speaker defers to the needs or ideas of the other person. But this type of overt communication is often accompanied by aggressive behavior. So, the person might say something apparently kind to you (although sometimes their tone gives them away), but then they say mean things about you or your idea behind your back. Or they may just harbor a building resentment toward you because they have a complaint that they are not telling you about. In the end, passive-aggressive communication tends to meet neither the needs of the speaker nor the needs of the other person.

We are hard-pressed to think of an example in which passive-aggressive communication would be desirable. Generally, we want to try to notice when we're doing it so we can think about whether there might be a more direct, helpful, or productive way of communicating or getting our needs met.

Aggressive communication is direct communication that makes it clear that one person has more power than the other and is imposing their will. This message might come out in overtly rude or mean language and/or tone, and it might be accompanied by intimidating body language as well. Statements such as, "That's wrong," "You're stupid," or "I don't need your approval; I'm doing it this way"—often spoken loudly—are aggressive.

Might you ever want to be aggressive? Yes. Consider a situation in which another person is violating your rights—perhaps violating your personal space or touching you inappropriately. We now teach our children to shout, "STOP!" when something like this happens, or "NO!" Is that aggressive? Not really, but it's hard for some of us to speak loudly and directly, even to protect ourselves, and it might serve us well to get more comfortable with this kind of communication for those situations in which it is necessary.

Many cultures value assertive communication. That doesn't mean it is always the best choice. How you want to communicate may depend on myriad factors, such as the cultures of the people engaging in the conversation, their roles, their gender, and the particular goals for the interaction. Still, many of us could stand to become more comfortable and practiced with assertive communication not because it is always objectively the best style, but because it can enable us to be more intentional about how we want to interact in a given situation.

ACTIVE LISTENING

You've probably heard of active listening. You may even have been trained in active listening. And even if you haven't been trained, we bet you can think of a situation in which it was *not* happening: You were talking and felt like the other person was very clearly not listening well. Consider Luke, the social worker, again (introduced in Chapter 1) and a situation he is dealing with at work. One of the clients on his caseload, an 87-year-old White cisgender man with dementia, is making racist comments to his nurse's aide, who is a 25-year-old, Black cisgender woman. When Luke discusses this matter with his supervisor, they cut him off halfway through his description of the problem. The supervisor is immediately defensive of the man and ignores Luke's concerns about the effects that this man's behavior is having on the aide. No resolution is made to decrease the racism experienced by the aide, and a few weeks later, she quits.

Active listening involves listening attentively and nonjudgmentally while communicating (often nonverbally) that you are paying attention. It differs from typical everyday conversation in that we don't jump in to share our own stories or reactions to what the other person is saying. You may find yourself saying, "Mmm" or "Mmm-hmm" while the other person is speaking, and you want to make sure you're looking at them and not engaged in anything else (e.g., checking your phone).

The therapeutic approach of *motivational interviewing*, which is used to elicit intrinsic motivation from a person who is struggling to make some sort of behavior change (e.g., quit smoking), has a useful acronym for key components of active listening: OARS. Here's what the letters stand for:

Open questions
Affirmations
Reflections
Summaries

Asking open questions is a great way to keep a conversation going and to learn more about what the person you're talking to thinks. *Open questions* are those that cannot be answered with "yes" or "no" but usually require a few more words to address. So rather than, "Do you like ice cream?" (which can be answered with a "yes" or a "no," although probably more often a "yes"!), you might ask, "What kinds of desserts do you enjoy?" Could the person respond with one word (e.g., "Cake")? Sure. But we tend not to. We tend to respond to this curiosity as an invitation to share something about ourselves: "Well, it depends. Generally, I prefer chocolate to nonchocolate, though I do appreciate really good fruity-pastry desserts, sometimes, too."

Affirmations emphasize the positive, and they help to build or strengthen a relationship. When you offer an affirmation, you comment on or highlight a strength that has come up in the conversation, whether explicitly or implicitly. For example, if someone says, "I'm usually an organized person, but right now I feel so scattered!" you may want to emphasize the organizational skills they have. Alternatively, you can provide an affirmation that maybe was not mentioned directly. For example, if a coworker says, "It is so hard to hear these terrible stories day in and day out," you might offer an affirmation by commenting on what an empathic and caring person they are. Affirmations are consistent with psychologist Carl Rogers's notion of unconditional positive regard, and they show the other person that we are listening and that we value them. Obviously, don't offer an affirmation if you can't do so in a genuine manner or if you think focusing on the positive might come across like you're dismissing the negative. Just where those lines are drawn may vary based on individuals and on culture. What, to some, seems like genuine positivity can, to others, seem artificial or like you're seeing through rose-colored glasses. However, in general terms, our brains evolved to focus more on the negative (threats), so it can be helpful to make an effort to focus a bit more on the positive.

Reflections are a way of letting your conversation partner know what you heard them say. You can reflect the "surface content" of what you heard ("You had a busy day!"), or you can reflect the emotion that you think you heard ("You're really frustrated"). You may or may not get it exactly right, and that's okay. Indeed, it may be more valuable to offer a reflection when we're not sure we understand because it gives the other person the opportunity to clarify or correct. Your accepting the feedback shows that you really want to get it right.

Summaries are reflections of multiple thoughts or ideas. In a summary, you reflect what you've heard over the course of a larger "chunk" of conversation: "So, you're feeling frustrated because it's really hard to stay organized in this context, and you're wondering how to get back to feeling on top of things. You have some ideas but are not sure where to start." Summaries show that you're listening and can also serve as a transition—to move the conversation forward.

Again, you may not use all of these skills in every conversation—but they can be tools to enhance your listening by focusing your interaction on your conversation partner and what they are trying to say. Returning to the example of Luke, if his supervisor had used active listening skills, Luke might have felt validated and heard, and, together, he and his supervisor might have been able to problem-solve to find a solution that was helpful to the nurse's aide and resulted in her staying in her job and not having to deal with racist comments.

Are you wondering about how this fits in with being assertive? How can you be assertive, if you're focusing on the other person and not inserting yourself into the conversation much? Well, these two things might occur separately. You might want to start with active listening to show you want to understand the other person's point of view. Then, once it's clear that you've understood (you've reflected the idea back, and the person has acknowledged that you've gotten it right), you can assertively state a different perspective.

Marcella (introduced in Chapter 3) often uses this type of strategy when canvassing for candidates. Although many of the people she interacts with are kind, respectful, and open to hearing what she has to say, she finds that a few people get angry when she speaks with them. Instead of pressing on with all of the reasons they "should" support the candidate she came to talk about, she spends time with these individuals and truly listens to their concerns and frustrations in an active and empathic manner. She finds that in the process of doing this, the individuals not only feel heard but also cool down a bit, and the situation doesn't tend to escalate. After they say their piece, she is assertive but not aggressive in her presentation of how the candidate would address their grievances, especially on issues on which they had found common ground. While Marcella leaves the conversation unsure as to whether the individuals would actually vote for the candidate she came out to support, she finds that she was able to truly connect and hear the other person. She also realizes they have a lot more in common than she would have initially thought. It is all about how she approaches the situation: If she goes in aggressive and pushes back, no one feels heard, and the differences between them appear bigger than they truly are.

Sometimes active listening is the only thing you'll need in a given interaction. Sometimes our friends, colleagues, or fellow volunteers just need to vent and know they've been heard. When someone is feeling frustrated or upset, and they tell someone who tries to "talk them out of it" or responds with their own frustrations, they tend not to feel very satisfied. Indeed, sometimes responding with your own similar experience may sound like you're trying to one-up the other person's negative experience (as in: "You think *that's* bad?!"), even if we don't mean it that way. Some of us tend to jump straight to problem solving when someone comes to us in distress. If the person dismisses your suggestions or reiterates their complaint, that might be a sign that they just want you to listen. Try switching to active listening and see how they react. The other person might enthusiastically endorse your reflection ("Yes, exactly!"), or they might appear a bit calmer and move on to something else. These are both signs that your attentive listening is helping them. Of course, you don't have to just guess what the other person most wants from you in a given situation; you can ask them what would be most helpful.

Let's consider another experience Marcella had: She was recently talking with a 31-year-old, Asian American cisgender female climate change activist whom she met at a rally; the activist was trying to learn the ropes of lobbying local state officials to facilitate clean air and water acts. After meeting with the state senator to discuss the proposal, the activist found that the senator wasn't open to her ideas and did not seem to be helpful with respect to steps to move forward. In fact, the senator dismissed her initiative as too "dreamy" and stated that the constituents would rather have money spent on improving roads. When the young activist came to Marcella disheartened after this interaction, Marcella found that her first instinct was to share her numerous stories of similar situations. She thought to herself, "This is a rookie mistake. There are so many more helpful strategies she can use to move her climate agenda forward." However, despite these thoughts, Marcella decided to stay focused on listening to the activist's story and helping her process her feelings. She remembered how important it is sometimes just to be heard by someone and to have space to process those feelings. When the time was right, Marcella could help this young activist problem solve, but at that moment, the activist just needed a space for her frustration, and Marcella provided that.

Often people are mostly seeking validation, whether they would put it that way or not. *Validation* is an extremely helpful "intervention" in that it helps the other person feel heard. It lets them know that their feelings are legitimate (as all feelings are). It may also lower the person's arousal and help them move on, as opposed to what Marsha Linehan calls an "unremitting focus on change" that can lead to more feelings of anxiety and anger, which, in turn, interfere with cognitive processing (Linehan, 1997, p. 387). It also strengthens relationships: When you validate someone's experience, you understand them better, and they know that you value them.

INTERRUPTIONS

Interruptions are, in some ways, the opposite of active listening—or at the least, they are one example of not-active-listening. Over the next few conversations you have, see if you can notice when people interrupt each other. (*Note:* The interrupter might be you!) People interrupt each other, cut each other off, and speak over each other all the time, especially in meetings or in conversations with more than one person (think: holiday meal). It happens in person, it happens on the phone or in videoconferences . . . it happens a lot.

And, of course, we would be remiss if we didn't acknowledge that some people get interrupted more than others, and some do more of the interrupting. Research shows that men interrupt women more than they interrupt other men. There are individual differences, here, too: Some of us come from families in which interrupting is the norm, and doing so shows your enthusiasm and passion. Often in families with this pattern, it's hard to get a word in if you *don't* interrupt, which means we are basically being socialized to interrupt when we have something to say. Others of us wouldn't dream of interrupting someone, whether or not we ever get to talk.

What can you do about this? Well, for starters, you can try not to interrupt others unless you deem it really necessary. For example, if you are running a meeting, and a topic is taking more time than you allotted or someone is going on a long tangent, and the rest of the group is getting visibly antsy, you might want to "redirect." Sometimes I (Dara) will say, "I'm just going to interrupt here because, unfortunately, we need to wrap up this topic . . ." or something like that (oddly, explicitly naming the fact that you are interrupting seems to make it a little less rude—perhaps because you're demonstrating your awareness of what you're doing). Even in these situations, ask yourself what is more important: staying on schedule/ not getting off on a topic or encouraging the person who is speaking. If the person who is speaking tends to dominate every meeting, the encouragement goal may not be important. But if it's someone whose voice hasn't been heard in this group for weeks or months (or ever), consider letting go of your intended schedule for the moment.

If you notice that you interrupt others a fair amount (and I [Dara], early in my career, noticed that I did this in meetings), see if you can become more aware in the moment of doing this and ask yourself why you might have done so. Perhaps you felt you had something to add that had to be added at exactly that moment before the topic changed. Maybe you felt you had to correct some misinformation before the conversation went down a path based on that misinformation. Would there have been a better way to handle this? If it's about worrying that the perfect moment for your comment will pass, can you wait anyway? When you do get a chance to speak, you might say, "I'd like to come back to what Priya said, a moment ago . . ." and reintroduce the topic. In so doing, you also give your colleague credit for saying what they said.

What if you are the person being interrupted? What can you do? We appreciate the models of some women in politics who might say, "I'm reclaiming my time" (perhaps not appropriate in all settings) or just "I'm speaking." Perhaps that feels a bit bold for the context you're in. After letting the other person finish or at least waiting for them to pause, you can also try something like, "I'd like to finish what I was saying before" or "I'd like to go back to _____ [topic]." Notice any automatic thoughts you might be having about saying these things. Is it passive-aggressive to say you'd like to finish what you were saying before because you are indirectly pointing out that you were interrupted? Is it aggressive to "interrupt back" and say, "I'm speaking," or is it asserting your own right to finish your thought? Would you interpret those comments in the same way coming from a cisgender heterosexual White man as from people who don't meet that description? Let's see if we can evaluate communication in a thorough, reflective way. And again, you can decide how to respond in an intentional way based on your priorities for that conversation or meeting or your role.

In addition to noticing patterns that involve you, try to notice patterns in the groups you're in. Are men frequently interrupting women and perhaps especially women of color? Are there people who never, ever speak? What can you do to help all voices get heard?

In some groups, just drawing this issue to people's attention may be enough (or at least a good start). If you are in charge of the meetings, you could make it an agenda item to talk about making sure all voices are heard, and you could point out that you've noticed that some people seem to contribute more than others in group discussions and that you'd like to make sure all voices are heard. Maybe those who do more of the talking or interrupting know they do it and will make an effort to stop. Not in charge of the meeting? You could ask whoever is if they would be willing to address this issue.

In many groups, though, just drawing attention to the issue will not be enough to solve the problem—and not because our coworkers have bad intentions but because habits don't typically change overnight. In this case, you might want to try something that involves a more concrete reminder. Some groups have a ball or some other object that the person who is speaking holds. When that person is done speaking, they look around to see who would like to talk next (maybe indicated by a raised hand), and they toss the ball to that person. Perhaps there are even interventions you could use in the moment if someone is being interrupted frequently. Take this exchange, for example:

> *Priya*: I know that other agencies sometimes address this by providing bus tokens to clients—
>
> *John*: —what we need to do is—
>
> *You*: Hang on a second, John. I want to hear the end of what Priya was saying. (*Then you could look back at Priya, and when she's done, perhaps acknowledge that John had something to say, too.*)

You might also approach the people who are being silenced or interrupted (or who just don't speak much) and ask them about it: "I notice you're pretty quiet in meetings. Is there anything I/we could do to make it easier for you to contribute, if you'd like to?" Maybe the person will tell you they're fine not contributing—and maybe they are. But, at a minimum, they'll know that you care about what they have to say. I (Dara) have sometimes supported quiet students in setting goals for themselves (e.g., say one thing per week or per class session). I remind them that the things they say don't have to be earth-shattering new insights (although often they are meaningful contributions to the conversation) and that they can even use their voices to agree with and support others, perhaps especially members of groups who are often silenced.

Sometimes there isn't a lot of "room" in meetings for these folks who may be quieter if there are other folks who tend to dominate the conversation. Can you do anything about that situation? We think you can. Obviously, you don't want to tell them they talk too much, but you might be able to get them on board with making more room for new voices. You can thank them for their contributions, express your appreciation for their ideas and for their active participation, and maybe enlist them as a partner in trying to hear what others have to say. See if they have ideas for how to go about making room for others in conversations. A collaborative approach may help them feel a bit of ownership over the plan and may encourage them to speak a bit less when they feel they can.

MOTIVATING OTHERS

Does part of your work involve persuading other people to do things? To vote, perhaps, or to recycle? Or do you need to convince your coworkers to switch to a different system of doing things, to serve on a committee, or to join you in a project? If so, whether you know it or not, you have probably been using some principles from social psychology. Indeed, there is a whole branch of psychology dedicated to "behavior change," and its tenets have worked their way into a variety of sociopolitical domains.

In psychotherapy, we often hope to facilitate some kind of change in behavior. Perhaps a client would like to stop smoking, start exercising, or adopt a meditation practice. Of course, public health and safety officials also want us to do certain things: Check our smoke detector batteries regularly, refrain from texting while driving, or get a vaccine. Companies want us to do particular things, too, ranging from using a device or an app regularly for ordering pizza and breadsticks to reusing our hotel towels before requesting new ones. In other words, people attempt to change other people's behavior all the time. Notice the next time you're being persuaded or encouraged to do something (or to stop doing something), what strategies are used, whether you find those strategies to be helpful or effective, and whether they rub you the wrong way. There is obviously some individual variability in how people react to these efforts or campaigns.

Next, we describe some strategies that have been shown to be effective and that we believe are more helpful than they are manipulative.

Implementation Intentions

Have you ever received a call or a visit from a canvasser in which they asked you what your plan was for voting? "Do you plan to vote on Tuesday?" "Yes, absolutely," you answer. "Great!" they reply. "What time will you go?" You think, "Um . . . why? Are you planning to follow me?" These questions can feel a little creepy and intrusive. But if you've ever been the one making the call or knocking on the door, you know that the list of questions goes on: What time? With whom? How will you get to the polls?

The reason for that string of questions is that we know from research on behavior change (and specifically on *implementation intentions,* which are if–then plans) that the more specific your plan is, the more likely you are to follow through on an intention (we mentioned this briefly in Chapter 3). Intentions are a prerequisite for a lot of behaviors: Before you stop smoking or start an exercise program, you generally have to intend to do so. But intentions are often insufficient to effect changes in behavior. Several factors increase the likelihood that a behavior will be changed, and having a specific plan is one of them.

Again, it is not the aim of this book to help you manipulate people into doing what you want them to do. But you may find yourself using some of these strategies without knowing exactly why. Perhaps you see folks bristle when you ask them if they'll bring their children with them when they vote. It may be helpful to you to know *why* you're being asked to ask these seemingly intrusive questions. And, of course, if someone tells you they intend to vote, encouraging them to make a specific plan is helping them accomplish what they themselves want to do. You can even be transparent about why you're doing so, thus giving them a bit of information they can use to help themselves reach other goals, too.

Perceived Value

People are not likely to make a change or an investment or adopt new behaviors or systems just because you want them to (unless you're their boss, in which case they might but possibly not with the enthusiasm you'd prefer). You need to explain clearly how the new thing is better—and how it's better for *them*. Chances are, you are not trying to engage people in some kind of a pyramid scheme or trying to scam them (probably scammers pick up other books). You perhaps really and truly believe the change or candidate or whatever it is will help the cause. Explain that.

Remember: Even if you are all on the same team, other people's priorities may not be exactly the same as yours. This is where your active listening comes in handy. What *is* the most important thing to the people you'd like to join you? To return to the canvassing example, this is why canvassers are often instructed to ask people what issues are most important to them in a given election. Of course, there are other reasons for collecting these data, too. But it probably doesn't help much if the voter's biggest concern is job creation, and the canvasser goes on and on about the environment—even if the voter and the candidate are actually on the same page about the environment. So, meet the other person where they are and show them how whatever you are "selling" will help them with what is important to them (again, assuming it will—we are not suggesting you lie!).

A Personal Approach

Don't worry—we're not suggesting that you ask intrusive questions (this time). Rather, we want to make the point that much of the time, personal anecdotes are more compelling than abstract numbers. This is why sometimes campaigns ask us for our "health care stories," and it explains why we remember the story of a man and his child who drowned trying to get to the United States more than we remember statistics for the numbers of people who die each year doing the same. And it's why ads for weight-loss programs show us "before" and "after" pictures of one person (sometimes a celebrity) rather than the results of the randomized clinical trial in which their program worked better than another one (if such data even exist).

You get the point. Tell people why *you* are invested in a cause—what it means to you. Let's consider the #MeToo movement. Tarana Burke is an American activist who is known as the founder of this movement. In 2006, she shared her own story about sexual violence with others and encouraged the women she met—also survivors of sexual assault—to share their stories and fight for justice by using the phrase and hashtag #MeToo. Nearly 11 years later, that phrase would go viral on social media as celebrities began to share their sexual assault stories. It's an excellent example of how sharing our stories can have a profound influence on others and society.

Why? Because individual stories involve emotional reactions. Statistics tend not to. They tend to be abstract, and we can deal with them on a purely intellectual level. Large numbers are also a bit hard to wrap our brains around. Individual stories ask us to relate and then evoke an emotional response. That is more likely to motivate us to do something.

Don't have a personal story to share or don't feel comfortable sharing yours? That's fine. Tell a story of someone you know (obviously without betraying their confidentiality in any way). "A friend of mine lost her job, so she lost her health care, and now their family is dealing with _____" is a fine way to begin and probably more compelling than stating the number of people who lost their health insurance in the past year. It's important to remember that the decision to share something personal and private is yours, and you should only do so if you feel ready to. You may never be ready to share that story for a variety of reasons, and that is okay (see the section on self-compassion in Chapter 8). You can still facilitate change without disclosing personal details of your life.

Constituents drive a lot of the decision making in our government by sharing their stories. In the book *Citizen's Handbook to Influencing Elected Officials*, the power of the story is nicely illustrated in the effect that different types of feedback have on legislator action. For example, they differentiate between the effects of a constituent's *opinion*—feeling strongly about something without a vested interest—and an *interest*—a strong feeling of someone who is impacted by the issue. A legislator may put more weight on input from someone who is directly impacted by an issue. For instance, think of issues related to the environment and a chemical spill in a region. Many constituents voice concerns about the spill and its impact on the environment. They are outraged because of the impact on the earth without it directly affecting them. However, if there are constituents who share their story about the way the spill has affected their drinking water and is the likely cause of the illness their child now has, that story has the power to have a greater influence on the decisions and behavior of the legislator.

So, when you can, consider sharing a personal story with as much or as little detail as you are comfortable sharing (certainly less is better if you're sharing someone else's story, unless they have explicitly given you permission to share more in support of the cause). Personal stories affect us more, as humans, than abstract information does.

Repetition

This one is fairly straightforward: The fact is, we don't remember everything that is said to us. So, if you want folks to remember something (say, the date of an important event or a candidate's name), you'll probably want to say it more than once. Sometimes we might think, "Oh, I already told them that" and not want to repeat ourselves. But, actually, you might well want to repeat yourself. One way to make it sound less repetitive (or at least less annoyingly repetitive) is to word something differently, the second time around. So instead of saying, "The day of action is on January 18th" twice, you might choose to say, "I hope to see you on the 18th!" the second time, instead.

This, we are sorry to say, is also why people sometimes send out multiple emails about the same thing. We may have to make personal decisions here about just how much we are willing to repeat ourselves in the service of whatever cause it is. I (Dara), for example, really *hate* what feels to me like "nagging." When I was department chair, I eventually made a conscious decision to stop nagging my coworkers about things I was supposed to get them to do, figuring that they were grown-ups who could take care of their own responsibilities (and, if not, the people who needed them to do the relevant tasks could follow up). I am pretty selective in nagging my family members and do so only when it's really important (although my family members might not agree with this characterization). In my social action/justice work, though, I am *somewhat* more willing to send a reminder email because I really believe in the cause in question. As with so many things, a cost-benefit analysis might be helpful in deciding just how much to remind people of what you want them to remember.

Handling Disagreements

Disagreements can be tough, and probably few of us consistently handle them as well as we'd like to. Of course, there is variation in how we respond to disagreements, and that's probably as it should be. Disagreeing with your business partner is different from disagreeing with your life partner. Disagreeing with your child is different from disagreeing with your parent. And, of course, there are probably individual differences based on how we saw disagreements happening as we were growing up and throughout our lives, too.

Once again, our goal here is intentionality: How do you *want* to handle disagreements? How do you want to handle each particular disagreement? You may want to come back to your identified values, here. What kind of a partner/employee/boss/organizer/friend/son do you want to be?

You have probably heard the advice: "Criticize the idea, not the person." You can certainly disagree with a person, but it is often helpful to try to keep the debate or discussion at the level of ideas rather than attack individuals themselves for what they have said ("You're such an idiot" vs. "I disagree"). This seems a reasonable place to start.

Part of the reason we may not be handling disagreements in ways that align closely with our values probably comes back to anxiety. Remember how we said that validation can lower arousal? Well, disagreement can feel invalidating and can increase anxiety. Do you notice that, in particular contexts, when someone says something you disagree with, you feel your heart rate go up or you suddenly feel pressure to respond instantly? That's what we're talking about. Disagreements can feel uncomfortable or threatening.

Why? Why might seeing things differently cause anxiety? Here's another good opportunity to tune into your thoughts. When you notice your anxiety increasing, ask yourself, "What just went through my head?" Perhaps you are having thoughts like, "I can't let that go unchallenged!" or "OMG, does everyone else think they're right and I'm wrong?" Sometimes these anxiety-producing thoughts might take the form of images or sometimes just short words or phrases (e.g., "Uh-oh . . ." or "Oh no . . .").

Are you catastrophizing? *Catastrophizing* is one of the hall-marks of anxiety: assuming the worst-case scenario. Sometimes this takes the form of a long chain of thoughts that begins with "What if . . .," like this one:

> What if everyone agrees with him and not me, and I just look dumb, and then everyone in this meeting thinks less of me, and they start going to him for advice all the time, and no one listens to my ideas anymore, and then I never get considered for promotion, and . . .?

Notice how, in each step of this "prediction," we are jumping to the worst possible outcome.

But sometimes we don't even spell all those outcomes out. Instead, we just think, "Oh no!" without really spending time think-ing about what the potential disaster is. One question you can ask yourself, if you have those somewhat panicky kinds of thoughts that a disaster is looming, might be, "Is this really an 'oh, no' situation? *Is* this a disaster?" And you might find it isn't. "What evidence do I have that this negative outcome is happening, or what evidence do I have that this is not happening?" (This is also a good place to invoke the "what's the best that could happen/worst that could happen/how would I cope with that?" line of questions or to use a relaxation exercise, such as taking some deep breaths; both strategies are described in more detail in Chapter 6.) It might make sense for you to take a break from the situation, to step out of the room, or to tell the person you'd like to come back to this conversation later. Once you feel calmer, you may feel better able to respond in the manner you would like.

What might that look like? Again, this is about responding intentionally, not about doing it "right." There may not be an ideal way to respond. But the more time you can buy yourself, rather than just respond impulsively, the more likely you are to be satisfied with your response. (*Note:* We do not guarantee that you'll be satisfied with the outcome of the situation. We can't control other people's responses.)

But what skills might you draw on here? Active listening comes to mind. And sometimes you might just want to listen actively. In other words, you might not always want to be trying to persuade the other person to adopt a particular perspective or to change their mind. Sometimes preserving the relationship is more important than persuading the other person. Also, sometimes your attempts at persuading the other person will cause them to dig their heels in more, so the attempts may be counterproductive. What if you just tried to listen and understand rather than convince? What would happen then?

Perhaps the ideas that the other person is espousing are so totally unacceptable to you that *not* arguing doesn't seem like an option that has integrity—in other words, you feel a moral obligation to speak up. Try thinking about it in phases. Perhaps listening and trying to understand is Phase I. After all, you'll do a better job of disputing the argument if you understand where the other person is coming from. And you will also have communicated to the person that you care enough to try to understand their perspective, which will go a long way toward building a relationship in which you can really discuss difficult topics.

In fact, you might want to start by checking to make sure you understood what the person said on a literal level: "I think I heard you say that people with mental illness are violent, but, actually, the statistics don't support that idea. Is that what you said?" If the person backtracks and says they "didn't mean it that way," you may want to point out that their intention is just one piece of the puzzle—the impact, or how what they've said "lands," is important to consider as well. You may have heard about this distinction between *intent* and *impact*, and hopefully they have, too. What a person means to say and how it is heard are two different things—and it is not only the speaker's intention that matters. How their words are received is important, and feeling offended cannot simply be dismissed as the listener's being "oversensitive." While feelings of shame and embarrassment may lead the speaker to become defensive, if you can maintain a calm demeanor, perhaps using skills described in Chapter 4, it may be a valuable lesson that affects the speaker's behavior and speech in the future.

Another strategy is to try to find *common ground*—beliefs or values that you do share with the other person, as Marcella did in her canvassing. A good place to start is sometimes with things that are believed to be universal to the human experience. Compassion meditation teaches us that we all want to be happy and free from suffering and that we all want to love and to be loved. In addition, we want our loved ones to be happy and free from suffering. Can you see how what your conversation partner is saying fits into that framework? Doing so might help you understand their point of view.

This is also a good time to think about communication style. If you do want to express your dissent, how do you want to do it? Remember that your goal is to help the person see your perspective, not to "be right." If you're someone who tends to get angry in these situations, you might want to make sure your language and tone are not aggressive. If you're someone who tends to hedge too much in the face of disagreement, practice stating some of your most deeply held beliefs out loud. State your beliefs in a direct and matter-of-fact way:

- I tend to believe people are generally good.
- I don't believe one group of people is less deserving than other groups of people.

- Actually, immigrants are responsible for proportionally less crime than people who were born here. (Sometimes what we are stating is an empirically verifiable fact, not just a belief.)
- I think the future of our planet should be our number one priority.

BOTTOM LINE

There is not one best way to communicate, but many of us would benefit from checking in to see if we are communicating in the way we think we are or intend to. Different situations, different people, and different contexts, including cultural contexts, might call for different responses. We hope you've gotten from this chapter ideas that might help you communicate in different ways so that you can be more intentional and nuanced in your approach to different situations to better meet your goals.

CHAPTER 6

GOING BEYOND YOUR COMFORT ZONE

Angelique pushed back tears as the acrid smell of smoke hit her nose. Another blaze, likely set by a cooking fire, had ignited along the river parkway. Someone Angelique knew had recently lost his business to a fire like this. People who were living along the river parkway were cooking outside because they didn't have stable housing. Rather than sit by helplessly as her business owner friend pulled himself together for a new start, Angelique decided to get involved.

A friend of Marcella's (we introduced Marcella in Chapter 3), Angelique, a 30-year-old, Caribbean American, cisgender woman, first explored small business groups to see if she could put her marketing skills to work to help business owners like her friend. This turned out not to be a good fit. Later, a friend who worked for the city put Angelique in touch with a housing advocacy group. Their most urgent need, which matched up nicely with Angelique's availability and desire to help, was data collection. Angelique agreed to join the organization's annual homeless census. After one evening on the job, she volunteered to help for the next three nights in a row or until the count was complete.

Unfortunately, when explaining to her family why she would need to trade evening dishwashing duty with someone else for the week, they reacted badly. They were angry that Angelique would shirk her family chore, but mainly, they felt that the cause wasn't worth her time. "How does counting homeless people solve anything?" they asked. Her uncle said, "Those people choose to live outside. They wanna be able to drink, and they know they can't do that in the shelters, and they wanna keep their vicious dogs with them, too." He went on, "If we want their cooking fires to quit burning up our city and their dogs to quit terrorizing people, we need to just let the police keep doing their job and clear out their illegal encampments."

Angelique didn't know what to say. She really didn't know how the "point in time" count data would be used or if her contribution would have any effect on whether police continued to clear the encampments. She believed that parts of what her uncle said weren't true; however, she couldn't imagine challenging him—she was brought up to not challenge elders. Her stomach sank when she remembered the woman she met on her first night of the count. That woman's car had been towed, and her grocery cart of extra clothing was gone. Where could she "move along" to, and how would she even get there? Angelique's heart started racing, thinking of how to respond to her uncle. Joining the homeless count was scary enough. Her uncle was right that a dog could jump out from behind a bush at any moment, ready to defend its owner. But what really made her palms sweat and her heart race was talking to people she loved about the work when they just weren't on the same page.

Angelique isn't alone in feeling this distress. Sometimes sharing with loved ones your passion and drive to make a difference can cause a lot of discomfort. Perhaps they don't agree with the cause we are fighting for, or, even worse, they are actively against it. These are often people we have shared many experiences with, and we might think our values are the same, so it can feel uncomfortable when we discover these differences. It can also be difficult if family members do feel the same way we do but won't pick up the slack at home so that we can do our social justice work. In this chapter, we discuss how to cope with different types of anxiety and frustration as we progress with our change-making.

As described in Chapter 1, building on our strengths can be a great way to start helping. On the other hand, you might find that the activities that you think may be most effective or meaningful also have the unfortunate feature of being things that make you anxious or are things you think about yourself as being "bad at" (e.g., "I'm bad at math," "I hate calling people on the phone"). In other words, your anxiety or your mindset (or both!) might be getting in the way of your doing the very work that would be most meaningful to you. Let's address these obstacles in turn.

FACING THE THINGS THAT SCARE YOU

You may find that you are not super gung ho about some of the activist activities available to you. Perhaps you get emails asking you to make cold calls to people in another state. Or maybe you are asked to serve on the board of your child's sports league, and while you know this means you'll have some opportunities to weigh in on important policies that could ensure the league better serves children and families, it's also likely that you'll be stuck wrangling snack bar volunteers most Saturdays instead of watching the games. You're not alone: *Many* people don't like these activities. Aversions to talking on the phone (particularly to strangers) can range from discomfort ordering pizza (and perhaps a preference for doing it online) to paralyzing anxiety about social situations that interferes with your life.

Either way, you have a choice about how to approach these situations. You may feel so compelled to get involved in whatever ways appear to be most effective that you decide to tackle these anxieties or discomforts and do them anyway. Or you might decide to focus your energies elsewhere. Again, there are many ways to get involved and to make a positive difference: You can write emails, letters, and postcards. You can participate in protests or organize community activities or participate in one that someone else has organized. You can deliver meals to folks who are homebound or participate in a cleanup on Earth Day. You can try to spend your time interacting with like-minded folks in a productive way if you find that talking to folks who disagree with you is stressful.

There are a lot of pressures out there about what we *should* be doing. As we've mentioned before, you may want to check these thoughts. *Should* according to whom? And who is supposed to do it? Although it's important to get better at talking to people with whom we disagree, that doesn't mean you personally have to jump at every opportunity to do it. But you could certainly give it a try and see how it goes.

Suppose you do decide to take part in a task that makes you anxious. How might you approach the event or task? Cognitive behavior therapy has a few strategies we might draw on, and we review several of them next.

The Relaxation Response

First described by Herbert Benson at Harvard in 1975, the *relaxation response* is a specific physiological reaction that counters the body's typical reaction to stress or anxiety (known as the fight-or-flight reaction). Have you ever felt your heart start racing when you get nervous? Or you suddenly feel sick to your stomach or like it's difficult to breathe? These can all be parts of the way the human body responds to threat. However, if our bodies react this way too much, we may end up with physical or emotional problems.

The relaxation response consists of decreasing heart rate and blood pressure, slowing breathing, and decreasing muscle tension.

As such, we recommend these explicit relaxation exercises for anxiety because they are incompatible with aspects of anxiety: Your heart rate cannot be both faster and slower at the same time. So, slowing it down directly counteracts these physiological aspects of the stress response. And, concurrently, the relaxation response works to decrease the psychological aspects of anxiety, too.

CONTROLLED BREATHING

So, how do we elicit this response? Several tried-and-true strategies have been used over and over in the context of many kinds of anxiety (and, indeed, many other kinds of distress), and they reliably give clients relief from anxiety symptoms. We start with *controlled breathing*, which you may have heard referred to as "deep breathing" or "diaphragmatic breathing" (perhaps you've even seen someone demonstrate this type of breathing while lying down: You see their abdomen go up and down as they breathe). Babies breathe this way—which suggests that we all did it, once. But throughout our lives, we shift to shallow breathing, so it's helpful to retrain ourselves in deeper, more controlled breathing.

This exercise has many variations, so you might want to try several to see which you like most. The same goes for all of the relaxation exercises—indeed, you may find that you like progressive muscle relaxation (PMR; we talk about this later) more than controlled breathing, or vice-versa. That's fine. Go with what you like because you'll be more likely to do it! In the appendix (in the Anxiety and Relaxation section), we've included information about exercises we really like. You can also find scripts for some of these exercises online, record yourself reading them (slowly and calmly), and then listen to them as you practice. Of note, some researchers believe that it is the "controlled" aspect of these breathing exercises that is key. So, it's important to actively controlling your breathing in some way: slowing it down, breathing more deeply, and so on.

That's not to say that exercises that ask you to focus on your normal or natural breathing are not helpful, but they may not have exactly the same effects as this type of exercise.

Another tip: Rate your anxiety on a scale of 0 (*no anxiety*) to 10 (*the most anxiety I've ever felt*—perhaps akin to a panic attack), before and after you do each of these exercises—every time. We'll come back to the reason for this in a bit.

Did you try one (or several)? You may have noticed a few potential "active ingredients" in that exercise. Slowing your breathing has the effect of slowing other things (e.g., heart rate). Controlling your breathing in this way may also give you a sense of increased control in general, which can be especially helpful if things in your life are feeling overwhelming and out of control. In addition, the focus on the breath may contain some elements of mindfulness. That helps us to shift our focus intentionally throughout the day to what is going on in the present instead of ruminating about past events or worrying about future ones. Focusing attention on the breath is an anchor to the present moment.

We recommend you try this exercise for a little while (a few days or a week) before moving on to the next one (although you can certainly read about them all now, if you like). Try practicing it at different times of day: when you first wake up, when you come home from work, or just before bed. If you practice every day (or almost every day) for a while, it will become more automatic, and you'll be able to use this strategy more or less whenever and wherever you are (e.g., on the bus, at a meeting). Obviously, don't close your eyes in situations in which it's not safe to do so—and don't get too relaxed while driving, either. This strategy is one you can "keep in your pocket" once you're practiced at it. Eventually, when you notice your anxiety starting to increase, you can just deepen your breathing or focus on a few breaths and then return to what you were doing in a more relaxed state.

Remember those 0-to-10 ratings we asked you to do? Do you see any patterns? First, do your ratings go down from before you do the exercise to after? If so, great! If not, maybe try changing something about how you do the exercise. Do you find your anxiety levels going down more when you practice at night than when you practice in the morning? Perhaps you want to practice at night for a little while, then. If your anxiety ratings are *not* going down as you practice this exercise, though, try another type of relaxation exercise and maybe try controlled breathing again at another moment in your life.

PROGRESSIVE MUSCLE RELAXATION

PMR is exactly what the name would suggest: a relaxation exercise in which you focus on particular skeletal muscles and relax them one at a time (or two at a time in the case of muscles in your arms and legs). The part that might seem less obvious is that before relaxing each muscle, you're actually going to tense each one. This is because our muscles can relax more from a state of tension than they can from a more neutral state. Also, the contrast between the tensed and relaxed states can help recognize what it feels like to have our muscles in those two states.

PMR often starts out much the way that controlled breathing does—and frequently with a few deep breaths. As with controlled breathing, you can find these exercises in a variety of places. Sometimes this is called PDMR for progressive *deep* muscle relaxation (again, see the link to a PMR exercise in the appendix). Try a few different exercises. See what you like. Don't forget to do your 0-to-10 ratings before and after so you can quantify how well the exercises are working (or not).

You might be thinking, "I'm not sure this one's as convenient as controlled breathing. I can take a few deep breaths on the bus or in a meeting, but I'm not sure I'll start tensing and relaxing my muscles in those places." Good news: If you practice this regularly (e.g., daily) for a while, you'll find that your ability to spontaneously relax your muscles improves—that is, you'll be able to relax your muscles pretty effectively without needing to tense them first. You may also get better at recognizing muscle tension, which means you may find yourself on the bus or in a meeting thinking, "Wow, my right shoulder is tense"—and be able to relax it. Perhaps you notice a lot of muscle tension in particular settings. Relaxing your muscles may help to relieve that tension as well as the more psychological aspects of anxiety.

If you're someone who typically carries a lot of your stress in your muscles (as tension), this exercise may be particularly beneficial to you.

Cognitive Reappraisal

The anxiety we have about particular tasks or challenges is often caused (or at least exacerbated) by particular automatic thoughts, as introduced in Chapter 3. Cognitive reappraisal can help us address and adjust those thoughts.

The first step is to tune into these thoughts. Remember that these thoughts are often referred to as automatic because they often occur quickly and without our awareness. Remember, too, that we can become aware of them by noticing when our anxiety is rising and asking ourselves, "What went through my head, just then?" Step 1, then, might be noticing when your anxiety rises. For many of us, this is a physiological reaction: You might feel like your heart rate is going up, or your heart is beating more loudly, or you're breathing more quickly. Perhaps what you notice is not so much physiological but is a pretty strong psychological urge to get out of the situation (sometimes accompanied by thoughts that justify this inclination:

"Why did I sign up for this? Are they counting on me? Seems like there are enough other people here that my time would be better spent doing something else").

Sometimes the thoughts that come before or with this anxiety are pretty thoroughly spelled out: "I'm going to knock on the door of someone who totally disagrees with me, and they're going to yell at me, and I'm going to feel horrible, and. . . ." (This, by the way, is an example of what Beck calls catastrophizing, a concept we described in Chapter 5.)

Sometimes the thoughts are more vague, or they take the form of images. Perhaps you have an image of yourself carrying a box of your belongings away from your desk after you've been fired or an image of standing in front of your boss, feeling horrible about yourself, while your boss asks you how you could ever have thought what you were doing was a good idea. These images can be vivid and feel very real.

So, what can we do about these thoughts? Well, some would argue that the best route is just to accept them—remind ourselves that we can't control our thoughts—and move on, and that is certainly one possibility. The acceptance route and the cognitive reappraisal route have an important thing in common, as we mentioned earlier: They both involve reminding ourselves that *just because we think something doesn't mean it's true*. One way to orient our brains in that direction is to ask ourselves three questions:

- What's the best that could happen?
- What's the worst that could happen?
- How would you cope if the worst happened?

The rationale behind posing these questions is that anxiety tends to be precipitated by particular types of thoughts oriented at something that *may* happen in the future. Specifically, when we feel anxious about something, it's often because (a) our brains jump to the worst-case scenario, and (b) we think we wouldn't be able to cope with the worst-case scenario. The three questions (and sometimes a fourth: "What's the most realistic outcome?") are designed to address these anxious habits of thought.

Let's return to Marcella. She's been thinking somewhat longingly about moving to a different department at work. Specifically, she would love to be more involved in policy work because she has recently come to believe that such work is the most efficient way to make change. Marcella is feeling a bit burned out in the work she's doing now, and she is really valued by everyone in the agency. She thinks they'd probably support her in making a move like this, if she asked them.

But there's a catch: The policy folks go to meetings with local government officials and give presentations. And nothing scares Marcella more. Sometimes she wakes up in the middle of the night from nightmares that she's supposed to present in a meeting like this, but she hasn't prepared and has no idea what to say. In the dreams, she's just standing there with nothing to say and with everyone staring at her, and she's pretty sure this is what would happen in real life, too.

As you can see, Marcella's worst-case scenario is that she would find herself in a situation in which she has to make a presentation and would freeze or have nothing prepared. (Question 2, "What's the worst that could happen?" is often the easiest for folks to answer because it's where their brain goes automatically.)

So, we pose Question 1: "What's the best that could happen?" Well, Marcella answers, the best that could happen is that she has really done her homework and has some well-thought-out suggestions that actually save the city money, and the folks from their office are thrilled and begin implementing these strategies.

Why, you may ask, do we pose this question? Is the best-case scenario really that much more likely than the worst-case scenario?

Not necessarily. The reason for posing this question is that when we're feeling anxious or panicky, we may forget that there even *are* possibilities other than the worst-case scenario. This question reminds us that we can have a more balanced view of the situation. It also may remind us of why we want to do this anxiety-provoking thing in the first place.

And, if the worst-case scenario were to happen, how would you cope with that? Remember that what often goes through our brains in moments of anxiety is "the worst will happen, and I couldn't cope with that" (although some or all of that thought is often implicit—that is, it may be outside of our awareness).

Okay, so suppose you do go to your presentation, and your mind goes blank (because probably you wouldn't have not prepared at all—that's more the stuff of nightmares). What would you do? Perhaps you would excuse yourself or take a drink of water and take some deep breaths. You would refer to your notes. Perhaps you would have written out the first couple sentences word for word to help you get going. So, you would read those and then carry on.

One way or another, Marcella *would* cope—we always do (you wouldn't be stuck in that spot for all eternity with the team staring at you). And it can be really reassuring to remind yourself of that. In addition, if you really think through your answer to the "How would you cope?" question, you will have a concrete plan or plans that should also reduce your anxiety about the situation.

Exposure

One of the signature behaviors associated with anxiety is avoidance. Anxiety and avoidance feed each other. Suppose you are afraid of heights, so you avoid them. The longer you avoid them ("I haven't been above the fourth floor of a building since 1992"), the scarier they seem. It's as though our brains are telling us that they must be really scary if we're working so hard to avoid them. Also, when we avoid things, we are missing out on opportunities to learn that they're not really as dangerous as we might think. When you do go up to the 85th floor of an office building and nothing bad happens, your brain gets data that contradict the fear. Avoiding the 85th floor means your brain does not get that information.

Exposure is one of those ideas that is part of the mainstream in catchy phrases about facing or confronting your fears. And that is the gist: You do need to confront your fears to conquer them.

For instance, when I (Jamie) started in my faculty position and had to teach two to three courses a semester, I realized I had debilitating social anxiety. Before every class, I could not eat; I would have overwhelming anxiety and feel sick to my stomach. I would spend hours prepping the night before each class. I feared I would be unable to answer a student's question and would get embarrassed. Sure, there were questions I didn't have the answer to, but it wasn't embarrassing; rather, I learned how to navigate it. Through exposure to the situation, I persevered.

Often, however, everyday life does not function well as exposure on its own. It seems that for exposure to "work," we have to learn from it. Specifically, we have to learn that we can tolerate the anxiety associated with these feared situations. And for that to transfer to the activities of our daily lives, we might need to learn it in a bunch of different contexts, at different times of day, with different people around, with different pressures, and so on. In other words, you need to practice a lot, with some frequency and in a number of different situations. If this sounds like a lot, you may well want to seek out a cognitive behavior therapist who is well versed in exposure therapy to help you along this journey.

With or without a therapist, you may want to create a "fear hierarchy." For example, folks with a fear of flying often grow to fear things they associate with flying (like going to the airport or packing a suitcase), but not as intensely as they fear flying itself. So, start with the things that induce smaller amounts of anxiety, and when you are tolerating those better, work your way up (although you may want to jump around a bit because saving the scariest activity for last may reinforce the idea that flying is terrifying or impossible). Does talking to your boss about moving departments seem really scary? Maybe start by talking to someone else about it. Get more comfortable with the topic.

Getting more comfortable with the topic may also serve as a rehearsal, another strategy you might want to use. When we know we're likely to be anxious in a situation, it can be helpful to overprepare. If you are going to take the step of talking to your boss (or even just making an appointment to talk to your boss), script out what you're going to say. Rehearse it—out loud—several times, perhaps until you've memorized it. Similarly, if it's your first time canvassing, see if you can get your hands on the materials and script in advance. Practice before you go. You'll feel better when you're doing it if you've spent some time with the content of what you're going to say.

And you know what? The more you do these things, the less frightening they become. So, by the time you get to your fourth or fifth house where someone answers the door, you may find you feel reasonably comfortable. And if you do this once a week, or even once a month, eventually you may wonder what it was that scared you about it. Or maybe it takes longer. But generally, the fear tends to subside. The feared act may never be your favorite, but the anxiety about does not need to be an insurmountable obstacle.

DEVELOPING NEW STRENGTHS

In Chapter 1, we talked about identifying and building on your strengths, which is, of course, a logical place to start. Did you find yourself, as you were making a list of your strengths and skills, saying, "Man, I wish I spoke Spanish better" or "I wish I knew how to cook," and so on? First of all, don't sell yourself short. Might your Spanish skills be good enough for you to lend an ear to immigrants who are worried about being deported? Or to accompany Spanish-speaking parents to their kids' back-to-school night to help them navigate? But also remember the "power of yet," a concept from growth mindset (described in the next section). Maybe your Spanish isn't good enough to work as an interpreter—yet. Maybe you're not a great chef—yet. How can you develop these skills?

Many of us can't just quit our jobs and reenroll in school to pursue another field altogether. If you can and you want to, that's awesome. But for the rest of us: Can you squeeze working on a new skill into your daily life? Perhaps listening to a language-learning app in the car on the way to work or when you walk or run in the neighborhood? Trying out one new recipe each weekend or even once a month? Perhaps you can make your next vacation a mindfulness retreat to work on your mindfulness practice. Be creative here. Attaining new skills won't just be useful to your social action work; it also feels great. Learning and growth contribute to happiness.

Growth Mindset

Perhaps you are avoiding particular activities because you believe them to be a poor match for your skills. You may hear about friends going to knock on people's doors or participating in phone banks and think, "I'm no good at that" or "I don't know enough about the issues to do that kind of thing."

Have you noticed there's typically not an audition for this type of work? Generally, political campaigns or nonprofit organizations let you make phone calls or knock on doors even if you are not a professional phone-caller or door-knocker! They also provide you with a script. The idea is this: It doesn't require a graduate degree or any particular personal talent. We can probably all do it well enough.

Still not convinced? Enter Carol Dweck's work on theories of intelligence. Dweck's theory suggests that we can think about intelligence (and other abilities) from two different points of view: (a) We can hold a *fixed mindset* in which we believe that these abilities are either present or absent more or less from birth—and there's not much we can do about it—or (b) we can have a *growth mindset* in which we believe that we might just not be particularly skilled at certain activities *yet*. You've probably figured out which of these approaches is associated with more positive outcomes: It's growth mindset. Believing that we can learn new skills increases the likelihood that we will. Is it a self-fulfilling prophecy? Maybe, in part: If you believe you can get better at something, you're more likely to work at it. Research supports many benefits of holding a growth mindset.

We are not saying that there is no such thing as individual differences in talents or abilities, nor is there a total lack of ceiling to what you can do. I (Dara) probably couldn't learn to speak accentless Arabic right now (in my 40s). But I probably could learn to speak some Arabic, at least sufficiently to communicate in a basic way. Similarly, I was never much of an athlete and probably won't be competing in any Olympics—ever. But I seem to have been able to learn the basics of ice skating enough (in my 40s) that I could skate around a rink with my kids without falling down very often. Imagine if I'd just said, "I can't ice skate" and then not tried (not trying is frequently the outcome of a fixed mindset). I would have missed out on skating outside with my kids at the Parc du Mont-Royal in Montréal!

Want an example that's more relevant than winter sports? Take canvassing. Have you ever done any canvassing? Knocking on people's doors and talking to them about political candidates or making sure they know where their voting place is and have a plan to vote? Remember from our discussion about behavioral experiments that I (Dara) did this in March 2018 even though I didn't want to? It sounded stressful and aversive, and I couldn't convince a single one of my friends to go with me, so I was going to be with strangers, trying this new thing that I feared. But I figured I could probably learn what I needed to learn to do it, and I felt compelled to do it.

When my group and I got to the campaign office, we got training. We had a script to work with (although we didn't have to stick to it verbatim). I was anxious at first and asked if I could start out with a canvassing partner. I "let" my partner go first (do the talking at the first house where someone answered), and then once I saw her do it, I realized, "I can probably do that." I also reminded myself that perhaps no interaction would go perfectly. I might forget to mention something, or someone might not want to talk to me, but that was okay and indeed par for the course. Were those things more likely to happen to me than to someone else? Probably not much more likely. And if so, so what? I was there doing the best I could. People who were more gifted at it might be knocking on doors, too, but they couldn't get to all of the houses.

I ended up having a supergood time. I really liked all the people I met, and my group's candidate won. It doesn't always go this way (the candidates and causes I've canvassed for do not always win). But I now know that I can do this work, and I even missed it during the pandemic, when I switched to phone banking. So, now it's a part of my repertoire. Do I still get anxious beforehand? Yes, a little. But I know I can handle it.

Angelique Practices Her Skills

Let's come back to Angelique. How might she apply some of the strategies we've talked about in this chapter? Well, after her uncle reacted so negatively to the work she was doing, she went upstairs and called Marcella. Marcella listened and talked her friend down. She knew what it was like to have family members who didn't approve of or agree with what you were doing. Once Angelique felt a bit calmer, Marcella suggested she think of ways to help herself stay calm(er) in these types of conversations. Angelique noted that the intentional breathing exercises she'd been doing had been really helpful in slowing down her heart rate and generally lowering her arousal. "But I can't just whip out my phone and start playing one of those at the dinner table!" she said to Marcella. Maybe not, but could she remember enough to take even just a few deep abdominal breaths while sitting there? Probably, Angelique admitted. Angelique thanked her friend for listening and reminding her of some strategies she could use, and they both got off the phone feeling good about their friendship and about the work they were doing to make the world a better place.

BOTTOM LINE

Dedicating your skills, training, and strengths to a cause has many benefits. It's valuable to the cause, and it will help you find meaning. But you may find that your background and skills are not the best fit for the kind of work that would be most meaningful to you at any given moment. In that case, see if you can shift to a growth mindset, address any anxiety you may have about the new activity, and off you go! In the next chapter, we start working on developing particular new skills that may be of use to you in your quest to make the world a better place.

CHAPTER 7

COLLABORATING FOR CHANGE: HARNESSING THE BENEFITS OF THE GROUP

Chances are good that the social action work you're doing involves working with other people. Sometimes a fair amount of the work can be done individually and on your own schedule, and certainly there are advantages to that. At the same time, it is advantageous to be in a group. For one, having company means you never have to feel alone—others there care about the same things you do and share the burden of making change in the world. Consider Angelique from Chapter 6: She is dealing with unsupportive family members as she tries to help people experiencing homelessness. Being around like-minded people who unite behind the cause of decreasing homelessness can help keep her motivated and even ignite more passion for the work she is doing. When she returns home from her census work, she finds she is less irritated with her uncle because she has had the validating experience of being around other volunteers who all share the same vision and hope for the future.

Groups can also make sometimes ungratifying tasks more pleasant and can increase your social network. Whether or not you spend your off-hours with your group, you now have connections who can help you advance your personal goals or offer professional pathways that will help you find leadership opportunities or different jobs in your area of interest.

One of the more obvious benefits of working with others is the accountability that comes with it. Say a person plans to make a set of phone calls at 2 p.m., but then when 2 p.m. rolls around, they don't feel like it; they can easily convince themself there's something more pressing they should do in that time. But if they have told someone else that they're going to make those calls at 2—or better yet, if both are making calls at the same time—the person is much more likely to stick to their plan. The two of them could get together in a conference room (or coffee shop or living room) to do particular tasks at a given time, or they could work in their own homes or offices but check in at the start or after 30 minutes, or even have a videoconference window open, where others are working, too. All will feel a sense of accountability to the others on the call.

So, you may want to work with a whole group at the same time, or you may want to work with a buddy (one of my [Dara's] students—and also a teacher I had recently—called these "accountabilibuddies"). Social pressures aren't always a good thing, but, at times, we can take advantage of them to help us meet our goals.

In addition, for many of us, social interaction in itself is rewarding. So even if it might technically be more efficient to go out canvassing by yourself, you might be more likely to do it longer, have more fun, and come back another day if you do it with a friend or partner. Carpooling is often fun. Sometimes even if you don't interact with the other people directly, just being part of a group of people that is working toward the same goal can be energizing.

Being with like-minded folks can be beneficial. Depending on where you live or the kind of work you do, you may feel isolated, alienated, or like you're facing an uphill battle. On social media, many of us live in echo chambers: We hear our own ideas reflected back to us on a regular basis. Some of our daily lives mirror that experience. But for others, they do not. We're not suggesting that you should only talk to like-minded people, but we are pointing out that spending some time with people who share your values can be validating and energizing; it also can help with feelings of overwhelm and demoralization. In addition, these types of interactions can be helpful to the helper: Consider the phone call Angelique made to Marcella (see Chapter 6) after feeling demoralized by her uncle's comments. Both Marcella and Angelique left that phone call feeling supported. It is both important and rewarding to give this kind of support and to receive it. Especially when our goals are ambitious, it can help to know we're not the only one working toward them. We are all part of a team—whether it's the team of folks we work with every day or a team of others around the world who are working toward the same broader goals.

SETTING GOALS

In a small town just north of Buffalo, New York, a local town Democratic committee met to discuss their slate of candidates for the upcoming midterms. While the stakes were fairly low because their town had a Republican stronghold, they still felt that they had to put their best possible slate of candidates forward. Anything was possible.

During this meeting, which was intended to decide who the committee would support for the ballot, an argument broke out between the committee chair, Charlotte, and another committee member, Wesley. Many of the committee members had good friends who were Republicans. Wesley wanted to put forth a Republican candidate for the slate because he thought, despite the difference in political affiliation, that they shared similar values. Also, because the Republicans had already picked their slate of candidates, Wesley thought this would be a good place for the candidate. The committee started to argue and unravel during the meeting. Even though they were in the local library, shouting erupted, and things got heated.

Wesley stormed out when he realized that the others were unwilling to budge and would rather go with no one on the slate than to have someone representing the other party on the ticket. After that meeting, many committee members quit, and no progress was made.

This situation highlights the importance of having clearly defined goals. The group had a goal of recruiting candidates for the upcoming election, but there was some disagreement about how this goal would be achieved as well as about the parameters of the goal.

Current forms of cognitive behavior therapy are very goal oriented—that is, they are focused on working toward a client's own goals for themselves. These could include anything from feeling less depressed to getting their GED, to improving their relationships with their children, to finding more meaning in their work. One of the strengths of evidence-based therapy is the emphasis on concrete and measurable goals (as mentioned in Chapter 2). So, for instance, to go back to the example of the group goal of getting candidates to run for elected positions, if your goal is just to fill a slate, that is one goal. If your goal is to fill the slate with only members of one party, that needs to be specified. The more specific and concrete the goal, the better. The goal is also measurable: The group would know by the end of the evening whether they had a slate (and whether it was limited to members of one party).

It is often helpful for groups or organizations to clarify their goals and to orient their work toward those goals. Many groups or organizations have mission statements that can serve this function—or at least get you started in identifying your group's goals.[1]

---

[1]The business world often distinguishes between concepts in this realm, such as mission and vision statements, goals, objectives, and strategies (e.g., Hofstrand, 2016). You can determine what level of specificity is ideal for your organization.

Whenever possible, as many group members should have input into the group's goals or at least into the goals toward which they themselves are working. Having input into your goals generally generates buy-in: When they are (at least in part) your own goals, you're more motivated to work toward them.

So, what makes for a good goal? It's really helpful when goals are concrete and measurable. Something like "reducing the harms associated with substance use" is a noble mission, but you're going to want to operationalize it into specific goals so you can be sure you're making progress. To make your goals concrete, you'll want to find the abstract words in your mission (e.g., "harms") and come up with examples of them (e.g., lost days of work, motor vehicle crashes, illnesses contracted through drug use, deaths from overdose). Then think about how those are measured and what might be a reasonable goal for reducing one or more of them. Perhaps "reduce overdose deaths by 20%" is a good goal for a particular period of time.

In the political world, campaigns often set goals of how many calls they want to make or how many doors they want to knock. Of course, winning an election might be the ultimate goal, but break it down: What are the steps you need to take to get there?

It may be impractical to involve every member of your group or team in all of these conversations, and that's fine. Perhaps you are the campaign manager or the chapter coordinator of a larger organization, and the national office or party hands down goals to you, or perhaps you run an agency that has had a mission statement since before you got there, and everyone seems pretty happy with it. You can encourage your team members to set their own goals ("Commit to knocking on 500 doors this summer!" or "Follow up with each client at least twice per month"), too.

Sometimes groups have trouble generating concrete and measurable goals because they are not on the same page regarding the overall goals or mission of the group. It may be worth shifting the conversation in that direction, if possible. Many groups fail to capitalize on members' energy because they don't spend time unifying over goals. Is the mission set in stone? Do you or others have authority over it? Or can it be revised from time to time with input from more of the folks who have an investment in your organization? It is especially important to make sure diverse voices are heard and that their input is represented in the group's work. Making room for diverse perspectives that can unite over a common goal is win for all involved. If you can't change your organization's mission, maybe you can help your coworkers figure out which parts they would like to focus on in their work and help them figure out how their own goals align with different parts of the mission in ways that may or may not be obvious at first.

Obviously, the answers to these questions will vary, and you may have pretty defined constraints within which you are working. If you are in a position to give folks some agency over their work, that's great. Doing so typically yields benefits in terms of personal investment, morale, and productivity. You will be much more effective and efficient if your goal is clear and formalized and you have buy-in from all members. For others of us, the focus on goals may look more like identifying our own goals and how they line up with the group's goals or finding a niche or an organization where that feels like a good fit. It's worth the time it takes to clarify these goals.

ADDRESSING OBSTACLES

How do you address obstacles or barriers in your work? A good first step is to identify—in specific terms—what the obstacles are. This might seem like a discouraging exercise, but it's important to identify precisely what the obstacles are so we can both (a) work to address them more effectively and (b) remind ourselves that they are specific and contained for those days when it feels like everything is working against us and the entire situation is hopeless.

Let's think about what obstacles Luke might encounter in his work. We've already identified one: too much paperwork (which takes time Luke would prefer to spend providing direct services). Luke also finds himself frustrated when the other parts of the system are under-resourced, and he can't help his clients promptly. For example, if he refers a client to an agency that might be able to help them find housing, but the client just ends up on hold for ages and then has to hang up to go to work, Luke feels like that referral was useless. Or if he is trying to encourage a client to seek medical care, and when the client finally calls a local clinic, the first appointment is in 3 months, Luke worries about whether the client's condition will deteriorate further in that time. So, now we have two obstacles:

- too much paperwork
- other agencies that are overwhelmed

What gets in the way of the work you and your teammates are trying to do? Sometimes the frustration feels so broad and overwhelming that it's hard to pinpoint exactly what is getting in the way of doing the work we so really want to do. In this case, it is sometimes helpful to think about the moments when you feel most frustrated and jot down exactly what happened. Maybe you are in the process of phone banking or reaching out to people to engage in a fundraiser for a local charity, and you feel frustrated by how few people respond to emails or answer the phone or the door. Perhaps you are a supervisor whose team seems to feel demoralized by administrative issues that get in the way of their doing the work that is most meaningful to them, as Luke does. Go ahead and list the things that pop up repeatedly, the sources of frustration for those you work with, the reasons people give up or quit, and the things that most annoy you about the work you do.

You may be noticing that some of these things seem (and may well be) beyond your control. The length of the wait-lists in local clinics, for example, may be something you feel helpless to fix. Hold that thought for a moment. At this stage, don't evaluate what does and doesn't belong on the list too much. We're going to come back to the topic of helping people deal with frustrations that are beyond their control, but first, let's make sure those things are really beyond our control.

The two obstacles Luke has listed seem like things he can't control: aspects of his job or of reality. Certainly, Luke can't just decide not to do the paperwork anymore, and if he asked his boss if he could be excused from the paperwork or if the agency could just not require so much paperwork, the answer is unlikely to be "yes."

But just to be sure, let's look a bit more closely. Have we really been as precise as we could in identifying these problems?

Solving Problems: Addressing the Obstacles Within Your Control

One cognitive behavioral approach to problem solving uses the acronym ITCH[2] with these four steps:

1. Identify the problem.
2. Think of solutions.
3. Choose a solution.
4. How did it work? (Evaluate the outcome.)

---

[2]This acronym was developed by Muñoz and colleagues (2020; see https://i4health.paloaltou.edu/downloads/CBT_Participant_English.pdf).

By listing the problems, we took the first step toward identifying them. But we're not done with that step. Let's make sure we have named the problems as precisely and accurately as we can. If one of the obstacles on your list is "not enough time," let's see if we can identify an aspect of that obstacle that *is* within our control—at least partly.

Luke's supervisor is aware that Luke and his teammates spend far more time than they would like on paperwork and that it's affecting morale. The supervisor can't just wave a magic wand and make the paperwork go away. But remember how we've defined the problem: It's not the fact that there is paperwork to do that is the problem (per se); rather, it's the fact that Luke and his teammates are spending more time on it than they would like.

Here's a place where Luke's supervisor could call a meeting or assign a team to problem solve this issue. Is there a way to make the paperwork take less time?

Step 2 in the problem-solving process is to think of solutions. Here, you want to encourage your team to generate solutions, no matter how outlandish they seem, without judging or eliminating possibilities—for the moment. This is hard for many of us; our judging brains may eliminate ideas before we've even fully formed them. And if they are fully formed in our heads, we may be reluctant to share them with others for fear of being judged by other people. This is where the process might work best in smaller groups (as opposed to with your whole agency or organization at once). But perhaps you really want to include everyone to generate as many ideas as possible. If that's the case, then instead of just one small group of people to work on this, perhaps you break into groups of three or four and problem solve in parallel. Then, each group can bring their best ideas (evaluated later in the process!) to the larger group.

Luke had previously decided he would manage paperwork by consolidating all of it to the afternoon hours rather than allow it to intrude on the hours when he was most actively working with clients. But after talking with coworkers, it's clear that solution will not work for everyone. What might Luke and his coworkers generate as possible solutions to the problem of their paperwork taking more time than they would like? Here are some ideas:

- Do the paperwork more sloppily. (Remember: We're not judging yet!)
- Put it all aside and do it when you have more time.
- Advocate for the forms to be digitized because typing is quicker than writing by hand. (This solution would also allow for copying and pasting standard text.)
- Investigate software platforms that prepopulate fields when appropriate. (At this stage, we don't have to figure out how to pay for things.)
- Share tips with each other for saving time on paperwork.
- Find out if administrative staff can help with some of the paperwork.

That's not a bad list, right?

The third step is to choose a solution to implement. So, here's where you *can* evaluate. Perhaps we eliminate the first two options pretty readily. Doing it more sloppily is obviously risky with respect to the legal and moral implications (unless you are being unnecessarily detailed in your paperwork, but then we might call that "summarize more"). And procrastinating may be risky, too, depending on what kind of paperwork it is. You might never get to it, or you might not remember the important issues by the time you get to it, or something serious might happen related to an issue you should have documented.

Once you've eliminated the solutions that don't seem reasonable to you, your task is to choose the solution that seems the most promising. If it's hard to get agreement on just one strategy, perhaps narrow it down to two or three and then pick the one you want to start with, perhaps based on ease of implementation, time to complete, or other practical factors. Maybe you can do two at once: One person in the group can find out if the forms can be digitized or if administrative staff can help, and the others start a forum for sharing tips among the staff and start looking into software platforms.

The "final" step of the problem-solving process is to ask: How did it work? Come back together after a solution has been tried and discuss whether it seems effective or viable. We put "final" in quotation marks because if your problem does not seem totally solved (and they are generally not), you may return to your list of viable solutions and select another, or perhaps return to the think-of-solutions phase and generate more possible approaches (this is sometimes easier once you've tried something and have had more ideas). So, the process may be iterative.

This process has many advantages. For one thing, identifying specific problems more precisely can help us to feel less overwhelmed by them and to look at them one at a time instead of as a big tangle of discouraging realities. The process also reminds us that we may be able to do some things about a stressful situation, which can go a long way if people are feeling helpless. And this problem-solving process is systematic and practical, allowing us to make what progress we can in an efficient way.

But what about when the obstacles are really not things you can control or change in any way? Perhaps agencies being overwhelmed when you refer people to them is an example of this. But before we conclude that, let's look closely at how we've identified the problem.

It's entirely possible that the agencies you work with *are* overwhelmed and have long wait-lists. But is that the problem that you and your team have, specifically? What if we frame the problem as being nowhere to refer clients? At first glance, that doesn't seem much better. Maybe you are working with a list of agencies that your organization has used for years, or maybe you are looking up resources online when a client needs something, so you feel like you have the latest information on what is available. Is it worth double-checking that? Could you or someone else compile a list of all the possible agencies, organizations, hotlines, referral services, nonprofits, and so on that your clients have access to whether in person or via phone or videoconference? The person or people working on this task could call each of the numbers to see what their status is: if they accept referrals from where you work, if they have wait-lists, if they can help with the problems your clients encounter, and so forth. Perhaps they will find that a new organization is available.

What we're trying to show here is that you might want to make sure a problem is really and truly beyond your control before you accept that it is. But what if it is? Certainly, that happens. There are limited resources in the world. What to do then?

Working With Thoughts for Obstacles Outside Your Control

Here's where you might want to help steer yourself and your peers toward more cognitive strategies. What kinds of thoughts are you having about the obstacle you're encountering? Do you hear a lot of hopelessness or helplessness? These are feelings that can lead to burnout. For example, perhaps Luke and his teammates frequently share their frustrations with each other, expressing things like these:

- "By the time my client gets an appointment, they'll have been evicted."
- "Why do we bother referring people anywhere if they can't ever get the help they need?"
- "Are we the only agency in this city that is actually trying to help people?"
- "Will we ever get enough staff to actually meet the need?"

Importantly, we're not asking you to "correct" these thoughts in terms of arguing their veracity. If you say to one of your team members, "Well, *some* people get the help they need!" that may not help. Your colleague is feeling frustrated, and you probably want to start by validating that (remember the bit on active listening in Chapter 5). And the situations they describe may be fairly reality based, unfortunately, even if a bit exaggerated. Perhaps at some point, it might help to try to have people be as accurate as possible about these challenges (not overstating them), but you might want to start with the helpfulness approach to cognitive reappraisal: Are these thoughts helpful?

You might feel like there are some paradoxes, here, and there may well be. For instance, it's great that your team members have each other for support and that they can share their frustrations with each other. But do you find that, in meetings, sometimes the sharing becomes complaining and that it snowballs out of control? That might not be helpful. See if you can identify the point at which it is no longer helpful and then redirect. Or if you run the meetings, you could decide to give 10 minutes to sharing frustrations and then try to problem-solve (if there are potential solutions) or reappraise or accept if there are not.

Reappraisal in this situation (also called "reframing") might look like just trying to tweak your team members' statements to make them a little less global and a little more precise—and you might not want to start with this. But if, little by little, you and your team can shift their thinking to be a bit more specific about the challenges, that will likely help. Even just a shift from

> "Why do we bother referring people anywhere if they can't ever get the help they need?"

to

> "It's so frustrating that people have to wait so long to get the help they need"

may help people feel slightly less demoralized and may also help them get more validating responses from others. And it might point you toward a different approach to the problem, too: How can we help our clients cope during the time they are waiting to get the instrumental assistance they need?

Obviously, aspects of this particular situation and many other situations are really and truly beyond our control. Indeed, many of us are doing the work we're doing to try to make the world a better place because of some pretty long-term, entrenched issues that are resistant to change and require the time, energy, and expertise of many people to make any kind of shift. How can we support each other in the face of things we *can't* change—at least not immediately?

There are a few options here. First, we might (eventually) use cognitive reappraisal (discussed in Chapter 3). Instead of focusing on our own helplessness, might it be helpful to remind ourselves that we are doing the best we can and that what we can do does make a difference? We don't want to encourage you to voice empty affirmations, especially not at the expense of validating your team members' frustrations. But is there a way to meaningfully and sincerely balance out the frustrations with reminders of, and gratitude for, what we *are* able to do? Perhaps have this conversation with your coworkers so that whatever you come up with feels genuine and meaningful to all of you.

COPING AND ACCEPTING

One classic finding in the coping literature is that problem-focused coping is generally more effective for things that are within your control, whereas emotion-focused coping is generally more effective for things that are not within your control. If, from the vantage point of the work you are doing, nothing can really be done about some of these obstacles, and the frustration is just building, it makes sense to take an approach that helps you cope with them rather than an approach that keeps fighting them. Of course, the picture is far more complicated than that once we consider the details of different situations, the roles of the people involved, the cultures and contexts within which these things are happening, and so on. But it isn't a bad rule to start with. In this framework, cognitive reappraisal can be considered *emotion-focused coping*: You're not necessarily focusing on changing an external reality; rather, you're focusing on trying to change the way you and others respond to it so as to engender less frustration, demoralization, and burnout.

In parallel, the idea of acceptance might be helpful here. In Chapter 4, we discussed "acceptance" as defined in acceptance and commitment therapy (ACT) as the opposite of experiential avoidance, which is when we try to escape or change our feelings or thoughts. Remember that this use of the word refers to internal experiences, not necessarily external situations. Practicing acceptance doesn't mean that the external situation is acceptable. The idea is more about letting yourself feel your own reactions to the situation and then figuring out what you can do about it. You may find that your colleagues are pretty resistant to reframing their frustrated thoughts about obstacles or that they find attempts to do so invalidating. In this case, accepting the potentially aversive emotions may be helpful, and your modeling acceptance of your own emotional reactions might help others do the same (more on modeling in a moment). In addition, you can communicate your acceptance of your team members' frustrations by using active listening and by validating their feelings, as described in Chapter 5.

Trying Different Levels of Work

If you find that you or your peers are deeply upset about one of the obstacles you can't really change in the work you are doing, you might want to think about other approaches to take. If the work you do is at the individual level, perhaps you might want to get involved at another level in your off time (or if your organization can incorporate it into the work week, so much the better!). Many mental health workers participate in activities for the National Alliance on Mental Illness or the American Foundation for Suicide Prevention's Out of the Darkness Walks, for example. Might something like these activities help you and your team members feel like you are doing something about the obstacles that trouble you? Or perhaps you do work at the systems level, working for an education nonprofit, and you might find it rewarding to volunteer as a tutor or literacy partner, to reconnect with individual students.

So many of the issues we work on are multilevel in this way. They likely will not be solved by individual interventions or policy interventions alone but, rather, by a multifaceted approach. This approach is embraced by the public health field and is often considered to be the most comprehensive way to approach complex issues. Knowing that we are intervening at other levels may help us (and our colleagues or team members) deal with the frustrations of the work we are doing.

RESPONDING TO OTHERS' EMOTIONS

I wonder how much of what weighs me down is not mine to carry.
　　　　　　　　—Attributed to Aditi, a goddess in Hinduism

If you are someone who tends to be really affected by others' emotional states and you work with other people, responding to their distressing emotions can be a very real struggle and an important part of being able to do the work that you do. Perhaps you work in a setting in which you provide direct client services or a lot of your colleagues are feeling burned out. Maybe you work at a phone bank, and someone you call tells you it's a lost cause or that they've given up and that you should, too.

How might you respond to these challenges? One response may lie in the concept of boundaries. In Chapter 8, we talk about boundaries with respect to how we spend our time. Boundaries can also be a useful concept when we're thinking about our own emotions with respect to others', especially for those of us who are particularly empathic. Some people have more solid boundaries than others when it comes to other people's emotional states. For some of us, those boundaries may be more porous. These differences may also be related to socialization and gender roles: Women have often been socialized to be more empathic than men. In her book *Set Boundaries, Find Peace: A Guide to Reclaiming Yourself*, Nedra Glover Tawwab (2021; listed in the Appendix) identifies and names different types of boundaries and the ways in which people violate them—if you are interested in reading more on this topic.

One way to think about boundaries is with respect to your own skin—or armor. If other people's despair just naturally and automatically becomes your despair such that you walk out of a meeting with a client feeling like you are in their life situation, you might think about some kind of visualization regarding your own skin as a barrier that protects you from the onslaught of these intense emotions or perhaps about wearing some armor when you go into sessions so that you can respond to the client in a way that is helpful to them and not devastating to you.

It is also the case that when you work to make change (and even when you don't), you may make people mad at you. Some of us find it extremely difficult to have other people mad at us. Both of us (Jamie and Dara) attended a workshop designed to encourage people (especially women and others whose voices are underrepresented) to write opinion pieces and submit them to newspapers. The organization that ran the workshop, the OpEd Project, has a saying that appears in various places on their website: "If you say things of consequence, there may be consequences. The alternative is to be inconsequential" (see https://www.theopedproject.org/).

So, in other words, angering others may be part of the package, and we may need to remind ourselves of that. It can be helpful in these situations to take a step back and examine where the anger is coming from, especially if we find ourselves feeling (very naturally) defensive. Anxiety about others' disapproval or anger, like other anxieties, does tend to lessen with exposure (experience). And, it follows that avoiding others' negative reactions will only make the anxiety worse. That may not be very encouraging. If other people's reactions to you are causing you a considerable amount of distress, this might be an opportunity to use one of the mood-management techniques described in Chapters 3 and 4. Can you engage in cognitive reappraisal? The situation would be the other person's being mad at you. What thoughts go through your head about that? Might there be more helpful ways to look at the situation? Alternatively, might we just accept that it feels uncomfortable to have someone else mad at you but remind ourselves that it doesn't mean we did something bad or that we are a bad person?

Broadly speaking, we can handle the feelings brought on by other people's emotional reactions the same way we handle any emotion. Cognitive reappraisal might help. Acceptance might help. Social support might help. It's amazing how often we miss opportunities to use these strategies (yes, even us, the authors of this book!). Are you having a reaction to the idea that you could try cognitive reappraisal? Well, what automatic thoughts are you having about it?

In Chapter 8, we discuss more ways to cope with the stress that comes along with making the world a better place—in the context of self-care strategies.

Reinforcement

Human beings, like other animals, respond to positive reinforcement. If we do something and we get a positive result, we do it again. If we do something and we get a negative result, we're less likely to do it again. In addition, an overall lack of positive reinforcement in one's life can lead to depression, so continuing to plug away with little sense of joy or accomplishment is not what you want for yourself or those around you.

And yet, sometimes that is what our work looks like. Changing the world is a long-term project; it tends not to happen overnight, and there are often many setbacks in the process. Candidates lose elections. Grants get rejected. Agencies lose funding.

How do we keep our justice work reinforcing in the face of realities like these? Well, there are a few possibilities.

One is to *insert* reinforcers. We do this when we're raising children (think: potty training), and we do this when we're trying to get ourselves to adopt a new habit (if I go to the gym three times this week, I can watch my favorite show over the weekend). People sometimes feel like this is silly or unnecessary for adults, but humans of all ages do respond to reinforcers, and why not make things more pleasant and enjoyable for yourself and your team?

Are you having any automatic thoughts about this approach? Are you thinking, "Grown-ups don't need rewards" or "My team would find this insulting" or "This work is its own reward"? Maybe. But we'd encourage you to check those thoughts and perhaps to do a behavioral experiment to see if they're accurate (i.e., try implementing some positive reinforcement and see what happens).

Assuming you've decided to give this a try, what form might it take? Some workplaces offer the chance to win a gift card to a local restaurant as a prize. Perhaps everyone who does a particular task by a certain date (make it one that people tend *not* to do promptly or without nudging) gets entered in a drawing to win a gift card to a restaurant? Maybe you can even get the gift card donated. Or maybe you offer swag related to your cause for the volunteer who recruits the most other volunteers or who knocks on the most doors or makes the most phone calls. Just mentioning the person's name publicly can serve as a reward. Even just tallying the number of whatever tasks are being completed can help your team see how much they've accomplished and can be reinforcing. You can draw a big thermometer on a white board in a common area to track things, or you can do so electronically on a dashboard or other platform. Could you propose some of these ideas to your colleagues?

We tend to think of reinforcers as being contingent on something, and it's useful to set them up that way. But in the behavioral theory of depression, people get depressed because there are too few positive things in their lives, period. You can think of this as being too few reinforcements for engaging in life, really, which can then drive people to engage less. Burnout can happen when individuals feel overworked and undervalued. So, feel free to just work to inject more positivity into your work, whether it's contingent on performance or not. You and some peers could schedule a happy hour or coffee meetup. Say thank you and express gratitude toward people doing the work with you. (*Note:* We are not suggesting you do these things instead of making systemic change. Remember that the focus of this book is on making just those changes. But these things might help, in conjunction.) These small gestures can make a big difference. Think creatively with your colleagues about what you can do to make the work more enjoyable.

About Modeling

There are several reasons why you may feel it's not totally appropriate to intervene with respect to frustrations or morale issues, or perhaps you've tried some of the ideas described earlier, and your team members are resistant to your input. The good news is, we learn an awful lot by watching others. So be mindful of the words you use when discussing the frustrations you experience in your work. Model good boundaries (described more in Chapter 8): Leave the office at the end of your workday and mention the nonwork things you do in your life (perhaps particularly the health-promoting ones, like spending time outdoors). Your modeling these things is helpful whether you are able to intervene more directly or not. It sends a mixed message when you promote healthy habits verbally but are obviously not practicing what you preach.

INCREASING EFFICIENCY

Maximizing productivity is a challenge for many of us, especially when it comes to working with others. Before we start thinking about ways to do this, we want to note that efficiency is not our *only* goal. There may be times when you sacrifice a bit of efficiency in the moment in the interest of morale, or to reduce turnover, or to keep people engaged. But other times, we notice inefficiencies and are not sure what to do about them. Many of us could stand to tune into this question more often to notice when we get off track or are duplicating efforts as well as to look for ways to increase efficiency.

In many cases, inefficiencies contribute to demoralization. Sometimes folks who are really driven and perhaps anxious about their work may have trouble being patient with others who need more time, and in those cases, counseling (or modeling) patience may be helpful. But in other cases, we may be working within systems that have been in place for a while without being questioned, and that could be improved. If you are a leader, it can be helpful to ask team members (perhaps especially new ones, who may have a fresh perspective) to let you know if they see room for improvement with respect to efficiency.

Some of the ideas in this section may be more relevant for people in positions of leadership in organizations. However, even if you are a once-a-month volunteer, your own behaviors or suggestions may sometimes help to make the organization's functioning more efficient. Of course, you may also find that there is wisdom in some of the organization's practices. Either way, we invite you to think about these topics to help maximize the effectiveness of your work.

For example, perhaps you have meetings at which you never get to all the items on your agenda. Or maybe you gather people to start an activity, and there are so many questions that it delays starting the activity, and some people start to get frustrated. If you are running these meetings, you may feel pulled in multiple directions: You want to let your team members express themselves and ask questions, but you feel it's taking too much time. We invite you to be creative, in these situations; there's no one right solution. But is there a way to provide more information outside of the meeting so that you can spend less time in the meeting covering it? Perhaps information could be sent by email (you've probably seen mugs and other gear that says, "Another meeting that could have been an email") so that you can spend more of the meeting interacting with each other?

Sometimes it's helpful to set specific times for different items on your agenda. If your meeting starts at 3:00 p.m., for example, perhaps you expect you won't *really* start on your agenda until 3:05 p.m. I (Dara) had a supervisor who started every meeting asking for "acknowledgments, expressions, and regrets" (at least, I think those were the three items)—and now I start meetings by asking for them. Staff would acknowledge others' accomplishments, from sharing that someone had submitted a paper for publication to noting that a client had been working really hard on quitting smoking, that week (without naming the client, of course). Expressions were often of gratitude to coworkers but also sometimes to people outside the room, and sometimes they were expressions of sadness or compassion for a struggle someone was experiencing. Some people leave time at the end of the meeting for announcements or to bring up topics that might be discussed at a later meeting. In between, you could determine roughly how much time you want to spend on each item. For example:

3:05: Acknowledgments, expressions, and regrets
3:10: Brief introduction of today's project[3]
3:15: Questions/get started (those who are ready to get started can do so)
3:50: Debrief, announcements

Notice that in this schedule, the group may split into two parts at 3:15: (a) those who have questions can stick around to ask them and have them answered, and (b) those who are ready to dive in can do so. There are other ways to "divide and conquer," too. Perhaps you can have multiple people answering questions in different spaces

---

[3]You may have sent information about the project around in advance or discussed it at a prior meeting. Still, not everyone will have read what you sent, and folks may not remember the last meeting so well (or may not have been there), so a brief summary can be helpful.

so that everyone with questions doesn't have to sit through everyone else's questions (although it is often helpful for folks to hear others' questions and the answers to them).

You can structure your work in many different ways. Deciding which one to use may involve a cost–benefit analysis of your particular situation. For example, let's suppose the issue you're facing is that once people start talking about a particular topic, they don't want to stop. You generously allot 25 minutes for a topic you know will elicit a lot of conversation, but it is never enough. You want to make sure all voices are heard, but you have other agenda items to address, too. You could

- cut discussion off at 25 minutes no matter what
- ask the group, near the end of the 25-minute period, if they would like to discuss for another 5 (or 10) minutes, and if so, see what other agenda items they think can wait until the next meeting (or decide that yourself, if you are running the meeting)
- move on to the next agenda item but let people know you will come back to this one if there is time at the end or that you will put it on the agenda for the next meeting
- consider creating a separate space for people to talk about this particular issue further or to share their thoughts about it with you (perhaps anonymously, if you are worried that some might not feel comfortable doing this directly)

The list goes on. How do you decide what to do? The answer will depend on the particulars of your situation. Do you feel the discussion is productive? If not, you might move on to the next item. Do you feel all voices are being heard? If not, then you might *not* move on to the next item; instead, you might grant more time. What is the culture of your group? Does the group need more time to talk and become more cohesive, or does it spend too much time talking and need help focusing on the tasks at hand? In other words, make sure you are saving time for the things that are most important. As author and journalist Oliver Burkeman noted in an interview with Joe Pinsker (2021; listed in the Appendix) in *The Atlantic* about his book *Four Thousand Weeks: Time Management for Mortals* (Burkeman, 2021), the goal is not to squeeze more and more of just anything into your life or your workday. It's to make more time for what is important.

BOTTOM LINE

Working with others involves particular challenges. Did some of the sections of this chapter resonate with you more than others? Everyone brings something different to the task. Think about what you'd like to prioritize (hint: It might line up with your values!). Perhaps you are superefficient, so you're good on that front, but sometimes you prioritize getting things done over morale, and you're thinking you might like a better balance between the two. Or you see a real need for improved efficiency in your group. In whichever ways seem most relevant to you, we hope that some of the tips in this chapter will help to make the work you do with others more effective, more meaningful, and more sustainable.

CHAPTER 8

SELF-CARE

Be kinder to yourself. And then let your kindness flood the world.
—Well-known quote by Pema Chödrön, a Buddhist nun

"Self-care" is one of those terms that our ancestors probably wouldn't recognize. In fact, I (Dara) first heard it during my interview for my clinical internship in 2003, when my to-be-supervisor mentioned that the work they did in the clinic was tough and asked what I did for self-care. "I knit," I replied, hoping that hobbies "counted" as self-care.

They do, of course. And in the years since, many of us have learned a lot about self-care. First of all, one strategy may not suffice for all of the stressors in one's life. Also, not everyone loves the term "self-care." Some feel it reflects the hyperindividualism that is present in U.S. culture and that we should really seek to build more "community care." Others argue that self-care puts more responsibility on people who are being treated unfairly in society, requiring them to make up for what really are systemic problems. For example, suggesting that folks who are treated inequitably at work should just do more yoga to cope with it does not address the root of the problem, and it places a burden on people who are already being unfairly burdened.

We wholeheartedly agree that (a) many in individualistic cultures (e.g., the United States) could stand to spend more time caring for others and that (b) societal problems are responsible for a lot of unnecessary stress that affects people in different and inequitable ways—and we, of course, support working toward systemic change. That's what this book is about, after all. But we think self-care can be helpful alongside this work. Why not intervene at multiple levels— the systems (working for change) level and individual (self-care) level—to try to improve quality of life?

JUAN'S STORY

Let's consider Juan. He is a 19-year-old Latino gay man and first-generation college student who is a member of his college's queer student group (QSG). The QSG is for activists and allies of people who identify as lesbian, gay, bisexual, transgender, queer or as other sexual orientations and gender identities. The main purpose of the QSG is to fight oppression and marginalization on their mostly White and midsized university campus.

Having two minoritized social identities has been a struggle for Juan because he faces discrimination on multiple fronts. He has yet to come out to his family for fear of being disowned and rejected. As a result of his own experiences and struggles, he wants to be a support to other college students who are facing similar challenges. He is an active member in the group who tries to push policies on campus and raise awareness of issues facing marginalized groups, yet he is feeling burned out by the daily microaggressions he experiences on campus and is struggling to manage his emotions about failed tasks and policies put forth by the group. As a result, he is feeling less motivated to do more for the group. The faculty advisor held a session this week in their QSG group on how to engage in self-care. This is when Juan realized that it may be important to take better care of himself and that it wasn't selfish to set boundaries and make time for that self-care.

Some of us may feel a little funny about self-care, feeling we don't have the time for it or that it's overly self-indulgent. Consider this: When our cognitive load is high, we are more prone to having implicit biases affect our behavior. In other words, when we have lots of demands on our brains, such as many things to keep track of or multiple worries, we are more prone to making decisions based on automatic processes, rather than intentional ones. Decreasing stress, then, should lead to decreased effects of implicit biases, and, indeed, initial research shows that this is the case. If you aren't motivated to decrease stress for your own purposes, then consider doing so to help you be the kind of person you strive to be. It may feel important to you to reduce stress because doing so will provide you with the cognitive and emotional resources to be better at the work you do to help others.

What we promote in this chapter are activities and behaviors that are nourishing and energizing—things that may help restore your resources when they are depleted so that you can continue to engage in your community and your life in the ways that you find meaningful. And of course, we emphasize the strategies that have research support for being helpful.

BOUNDARIES

We talked about different types of boundaries earlier in the book, and we return now to the topic of time-related boundaries, which can be really important to self-care. Perhaps you are exhausted and feel like you need to take a break. Taking a break is often a good idea. But is there anything we can learn from our recent feelings of overwhelm, or any particular way we can spend the time away, that will be helpful in the future?

There are certainly instances in which it's not possible to set firm boundaries: Perhaps you are the primary caregiver for a parent with dementia or a child with disabilities. However, we challenge you to think of a way to take a break, even a small one. Could it be calling on a close friend or relative to watch your child for an hour so you can do something for you? Are there free public spaces like parks, where you can take a walk or eat your lunch? For some of us, "tapping out" is not an option; sometimes, just by who we are, we are engaged in social justice work just walking out of our home. How might you get a break from being "on" all the time in that way? Consider spending more dedicated time with others with whom you feel you can let down your guard: your closest friends, family, or community.

Social action, like many kinds of work, is often best served by reflecting on just how engaged or invested we want to be and in what ways. I (Dara) had a conversation with a colleague about this recently with respect to work. The colleague was reporting a need for a little more distance or space from some demoralizing things that were happening at work. I suggested trying to find a level of detachment, and my colleague said, "Then I won't know what's going on, and it feels really important."

That's the rub, right? But is there a way to remain informed without being quite as emotionally invested? See if this applies to your social engagement. Can you stay informed and involved but keep your work and the issues contained in some way? Can you check the news in the evening (or the morning) but only at that one time—and perhaps stay away from online comments? Or set a timer, and when it goes off, you shift gears and do something else? Limit your social media use to one time a day, say, from 7 p.m. to 8 p.m.? Can you put your phone and communication with work on hold between 5 p.m. and 8 p.m. so you can spend time with your family?

Boundaries can be about time or setting or topic or something else entirely. For example, if the issue you feel most passionately about is health care, you could schedule specific times in your week to get up to speed on the latest developments. Or perhaps you do want to follow the news as it comes out, but you find yourself doing most of your reading about it at night before bed. That means you go to bed feeling angry, frustrated, or hopeless, and it's interfering with your sleep.

How can you contain your engagement? There are all kinds of options. For one thing, you can try to engage less or even disconnect entirely. Maybe for a week or so, you stay off of social media or don't click on any emails related to health care. It's okay do this—you are not *solely* responsible for making change, and your coworkers or community members can probably keep things moving for a week without you.

But perhaps you don't want to do that. Let's say that you don't want to dial back your involvement at all. You just want to be able to sleep at night. Can you shift your social media or email time? Maybe wake up a bit earlier or even get to your desk earlier so you can catch up before the day gets rolling? Or at lunchtime? Could you then replace social media or news time in the evenings with something that is relaxing and helps settle your mind? When was the last time you read a good novel or worked on a puzzle? This might be a good time to pick back up the knitting or model airplane kit. There are lots of things to do that can help provide not only a distraction but also enjoyment.

You may also want to try something in between: Dial back your involvement a *little*. Stay up-to-date, continue to attend meetings and rallies, keep writing a community grant or building a curriculum for children in underresourced schools—but maybe focus more. Pick one event to attend each month and decide that if you're going to attend a second event, it had better be *really* important (and perhaps time sensitive—something you can't do next month). As we discuss in Chapter 9 on maintaining motivation, sometimes doing less and dialing it back a bit can actually help keep the momentum going.

Boundaries can also be about learning to say no. Often, people involved in social justice work, whether as a career or not, are highly involved and frequently sought out to "help with things" because of their passion, skills, and dedication. As a result, these people are likely to get asked to do a lot, and it can be hard to say no. Deciding what is a good use of your time and what is likely to be the most rewarding to you will help you prioritize and figure out which activities to decline. It may be helpful to practice either saying no or coming up with a phrase to use when asked to take on yet another thing, such as: "That sounds interesting. Let me think about it."

A challenge that Juan faced as he tried to increase self-care was setting boundaries with the other members of the QSG. A group chat set up when they formed the group started out as a great place to vent and discuss issues they were seeing and dealing with on campus. The chat helped to keep Juan informed, and he was able to be a support to his friends in the group. However, lately, when he hears his phone ding with another chat from the group, he finds himself cringe because he knows it is a group member venting about an issue. While he wants to support his friends, he finds that the messages bring him out of the moment and away from homework or relaxation time and remind him of all of the injustices in the world. He knows this is contributing a lot to his feelings of being worn out with the group's work.

One strategy Juan has been using to help set boundaries with the group is to shut off notifications for the chat so he can tune into the chat on his own terms. He makes a point to check it once a day. As a result, he has found his mood to be more positive and is less drained during his relaxation or work time. In addition to containing the difficult emotions that the chat can elicit, turning off notifications and reading the messages on his own schedule allows Juan to feel a little bit of control over what had become a barrage of stressful reminders.

There is also the struggle of maintaining boundaries with people who push your boundaries. Perhaps they grew up in homes in which there were no boundaries, or they feel their needs are so important that they push to get them met without respecting your needs and space. Luke (introduced in Chapter 1) experienced this with a friend at work. His coworker regularly came into his office to discuss issues with clients and in that person's own personal life. At first, Luke tried to be a good listener and colleague, but after a while, it became very clear that the more he gave, the more his coworker expected. They started showing up in his office with their lunch to eat with Luke. It got to the point where he didn't feel that he could get his work done, and he began to think about bringing his work home with him to catch up because these conversations were taking up so much of his workday.

When Luke had that thought, he realized the situation was a bit ridiculous. He had time to get his work done during normal working hours, and there was no need to bring it home with him. He decided to have a conversation with his coworker and set parameters around their interactions: When his office door was shut, that meant he was working and needed time to complete important tasks. When his door was open, he could chat. He also mentioned that he enjoyed lunches alone because it was his only time to catch up with friends on social media. While his coworker seemed a little sad when he shared this with them, they did respect it, and after a week or two, the new arrangement worked very well for Luke.

Defining your boundaries and committing to a plan to maintain them is one approach to managing some of the emotions that can come along with difficult work. Nedra Glover Tawwab's book (listed in the appendix) may be a helpful resource as you work on your boundaries.

PHYSICAL ACTIVITY

Yes, we know: Physical activity is not everyone's favorite topic, and we all know we should do it—or do more of it. But just in case, let's review some of the many benefits of exercise: Physical activity is beneficial to your physical health and your mental health. For instance, regular physical exercise can help with weight management and reduce your risk of cardiovascular disease, diabetes, and certain types of cancer. It can decrease the risk of early mortality. It slows the loss of bone density, lowers the risk of hip fractures, and reduces the risk of falling. In terms of its effects on mental health, regular physical activity is associated with increased cognitive functioning, improved sleep, and decreased depression and anxiety. There are obviously lots of reasons *to* exercise, but it's often hard to get started or stay on a regular schedule.

Bear in mind: Exercise doesn't have to mean going to the gym and using machines for an hour. It can, and that works well for some people for some time periods. But it's not an option that's available to everyone, and even if you have it available for you, it might not be working for you right now. Perhaps you have an injury that means you can't use your favorite machine, or perhaps you just have trouble sticking with the gym. There are, of course, ways to increase the likelihood of following through on a plan to go to the gym. (Remember implementation intentions? Plan it in your schedule the way you would a meeting, or perhaps make use of behavior principles and reward yourself each time you go or each week that you go a certain number of times.) Maybe certain forms of exercise or physical activity work better for you, or you enjoy them more, and that will make it easier to follow through on your intentions to work more physical activity into your daily life for the long run. Increasing exercise may also mean that you are trying to get 10,000 steps a day or starting where you are and getting 5,000 steps. Movement of any kind is generally good for health and well-being.

It's also important to remember that meeting your physical activity goals does not have to be done in one sitting. That is, you can break them down into smaller chunks and still reap health benefits. If you only have 10 minutes, go for a 10-minute walk or ride your bike. Even small bursts of physical activity throughout the day that are not done all in one "sitting" can be beneficial to your health. This is especially important to keep in mind if you have limited time.

Some people may be motivated by the direct physical and mental health benefits of the activity, but what if we said it can also help you be better at the work you do? Consider walking or physical activity as an opportunity to get a change in scenery, which can help you gain perspective in your work, give you an opportunity to see a problem in a new light, or think about something other than your job or social justice activities. Not only can this physical activity help lower stress and anxiety, but it can also help you come back to the work with some renewed energy and fresh ideas. Heck, it could also fill your patience bucket a little more, helping you deal with some challenging situations in your life.

You should first, though, talk to a doctor or other medical professional about what kind of exercise is a good fit for you and how much is right for you. Then, work up to those goals. Start small. Set achievable goals for yourself. And remember that not all exercise has to look like the image we may have in our heads of exercise. Take the stairs instead of the elevator if it's safe to do so. Get off the bus one stop early and walk the rest of the way to work. Park farther away from the store to get in a few extra steps. Go for a walk at lunchtime or when you're stuck on a task at work (it is amazing how much this can help!). Be creative. It's all too easy to find excuses to not exercise ("I usually take a walk, but it's raining, so I can't"). You can walk inside. You can walk around your apartment, the hallway of your building, or a floor of your house.

Another way to help with motivation can be to start recording your stress and mood before the exercise and after completing it. Consider this a behavioral experiment to see how the exercise is really helping you—by measuring it. We mention this idea of doing pre- and postactivity ratings of your mood (or other desired outcome) in a few places in the book. Understanding how various activities impact you can help you figure out which strategies or activities to use when. And seeing those concrete numbers (e.g., noting that your anxiety goes from a 7 to a 4) can motivate you to keep going with a behavior, such as exercise, that might not always seem inherently appealing.

Another thing to keep in mind is that what works best for you in terms of exercise may change over time (as with other self-care habits). Maybe you discover you love running and do that for years, but you develop an injury or other problem that makes running impossible for a while. Perhaps you have access to a pool during that period, so you start swimming in the mornings before work. Maybe you discover you love swimming so much that you stick with it for years. If you find over time you are loving it less, try other things. What about kickboxing? Have you ever considered taking a tennis lesson? Tap dance classes? If your motivation is lower in the dead of winter (perhaps you deal with several inches or feet of snow), try cross-country or downhill skiing or snowshoeing. Have you ever ice-skated? Trying new things not only count as exercise but can also give you the opportunity to challenge yourself and help you incorporate new (and possibly exciting) things into your life.

Social support and accountability can help motivation. Ask your neighbor to go for an evening walk and make it a part of your routine. You can accomplish two goals with one activity: getting social support by chatting with your neighbor about life and getting more activity in. I (Dara) and one of my co-organizers often have "walking meetings" in which we walk around the neighborhood and discuss priorities for the group we run. Have you ever considered setting a goal or joining one of the many fitness challenges out there? Do what works and keep moving.

SLEEP

Sleep and physical activity work as partners and are foundational pillars of health and well-being. Increased physical activity often helps with sleep, and getting enough sleep means we have more energy and motivation for exercise. So many of us shortchange our sleep, to get more done. At the end of this chapter, we come back to the idea of doing less, but for now, consider some reminders about sleep.

Lack of sleep can contribute to decreased immune function and can lead to weight gain. You've probably noticed that insufficient or poor-quality sleep can affect your mood (maybe you get a little more cranky or easily tearful) and can make it hard to concentrate. Did you also know that sleep deprivation increases your odds of causing a motor vehicle crash? We're not pointing that out to raise your anxiety (although it raises ours!) but rather in the hope that it encourages you to give yourself permission to prioritize sleep.

You can't force sleep to come, as we have probably all discovered. Indeed, some recommend avoiding the phrase "go to sleep" in favor of a framing like "let sleep come." Either way, most adults need 7 to 8 hours of quality sleep a night, and we don't always get it. Fortunately, we can frequently make minor adjustments to improve our sleep (or to increase the likelihood of getting quality sleep). If you're simply not giving yourself an opportunity for 7 to 8 hours or sleep (if you are, say, not going to bed before midnight and then you wake up to an alarm at 6 a.m.), see what's getting in the way. Are you up late reading the news or scrolling through social media or maybe watching TV? I (Dara) often find I'm scrolling through social media as though I'll eventually have looked at all of the posts and be done. News flash: There is no "done." If you find yourself scrolling mindlessly, you might just want to close your laptop or turn off your phone.

Are you doing work, thinking, "I just need to get this done"? Maybe, sometimes, we need to do that at the expense of sleep. But remember that your concentration may suffer if you don't get enough sleep, so you may be less productive the next day. Might it make more sense, in many instances, to go to sleep, setting yourself up to be more efficient the next day?

Maybe you get into bed at a reasonable hour, but your mind is racing. Think about what you're doing just before bed. Are you exercising? Exercise is great for sleep—but not right before it. Are you working up until you brush your teeth and climb under the covers? You may need more of a transition than that—more of a wind down period in which you do something that engages your brain on less stressful topics (e.g., reading relaxing fiction, preferably not on a screen). A short meditation can also be beneficial.

Let's come back to Marcella (introduced in Chapter 3) because sleep is something she struggles with. She is finding it difficult to sleep because she keeps thinking about asking to get more involved in policy work at her job. She struggles to shut down her brain at night because she is thinking a lot about changing careers and doing work she thinks would have more of an effect on the world—but also might cause her more anxiety. It's been tiring, and it's starting to affect her mood and ability to concentrate during the day. She finds herself getting frustrated as she tosses and turns for what feels like hours.

It's often hard for people to go straight from an engaging activity to bed, even if you find yourself exhausted, so our first advice for Marcella would be to take some time to decompress before getting to bed. Second, avoid tossing and turning in bed. If you find yourself awake during the night for more than, say, 20 minutes, it's important to get out of bed (even if you are exhausted) and engage in a calming activity like reading a book (some schools of thought suggest you should read a boring book, like a dictionary, if you have one).

This calming activity is to help get you drowsy or to feel what's called "sleep pressure" to increase the likelihood that sleep will come when you get back in bed. It's important to get out of bed, as hard as that can be, so you don't start to associate your bed with being awake (and frustrated). And try to avoid screens during these times; studies suggest that blue light from screens may suppress the release of melatonin, a hormone released in our bodies before we fall asleep, with levels increasing after that. When melatonin is suppressed, we may have difficulty getting to sleep and staying asleep.

The environment in your bedroom is important, too. It is recommended to make sure the room is dark and that the temperature is conducive to sleeping. You can find more information about these and other tips to improve sleep by searching the term "sleep hygiene" online or through the resources in the appendix. These suggestions often include things like limiting screen use before bed and limiting stimulant use (including caffeine) late in the day.

COMPASSION AND SELF-COMPASSION

If you are committed to making the world a better place, chances are, you're a pretty compassionate person. Thank you. We are grateful for you and your compassion! You might think, as a compassionate person, that you don't need to spend too much time thinking about your compassion for other people or that it might not help you to do so. If you look up the etymology of the word "compassion," you'll find it comes from a word that means "suffer with"—and you might well take in enough (or more than enough) of the suffering in the world as it is. Perhaps that is why you are reading this chapter on self-care.

It turns out that compassion training and compassion meditation can help you manage the feelings that come from taking in others' suffering. You've probably heard the term "compassion fatigue" to refer to exhaustion that comes from taking in too much of other people's pain. Compassion experts think that term should really be "empathy fatigue": *Empathy* refers to feeling others' pain; *compassion* often involves empathy but is mainly characterized by a strong desire to alleviate suffering and by action geared toward doing so. You may already be doing those things. But when people engage in formal compassion meditation practice, it often becomes easier to stay present with suffering. Compassion helps us to see things from a different (sometimes calmer) point of view and is considered a renewable resource. You might think of formal compassion training and practice as helping you approach compassionate action from a healthier, more sustainable place.

Compassion training consists of learning contemplative practices geared to enhancing positive feelings toward others while in a state of quiet concentration. Research suggests that compassion training can enhance positive feelings, whereas empathy training may increase negative feelings. Compassion is associated with feelings of warmth, strength, groundedness, and openness—not feelings we associate with burnout or empathy fatigue.

Another important question with respect to self-care is whether you treat yourself with as much kindness and compassion as you direct toward others. For some of us, this is extremely hard. Self-compassion is about being kind and understanding toward ourselves, even when we fail, suffer, or find ourselves struggling. This practice is in direct contrast to being harsh and self-critical toward ourselves. Some of us may have grown up in critical home environments in which we were always told (whether directly or indirectly) that what we did wasn't good enough or that we failed. Even if we didn't receive those messages growing up, they are out there, and we may internalize them, criticizing ourselves harshly when we make mistakes or even just when we don't live up to our own standards. Is that kind of self-criticism helpful? There are so many challenges in social action work; we don't think we need to add internal criticism or judgment to that mix.

Let's return to Juan, who is still struggling with sharing his sexual orientation with his family. He finds that he speaks harshly to himself when he considers sharing his identity with his family ("I am stupid for not saying anything. I should be braver and just tell them. I hate myself for being this way. I should man up"). A lot of the messages he says to himself mirror what his father told him while growing up. One of the exercises that he found most beneficial in the self-care session with his faculty advisor was on self-compassion. He didn't realize just how harsh and mean he was being to himself until that lesson. He now practices self-compassion meditations daily to help him work toward self-acceptance and self-kindness. *Self-compassion* involves self-kindness, being supportive and encouraging toward ourselves. It involves elements of mindfulness and being open to the reality of our experiences. It includes a focus on a common humanity in which we acknowledge that we are not alone in our suffering. All people are flawed and experience failings, mistakes, and hardships; those experiences are some of the things all humans have in common.

Some forms of compassion meditation start by having us focus on other people and, direct compassion toward them, often by reminding ourselves that they (too) want to be happy and free from suffering and that they (too) want these things for their loved ones. You may focus these thoughts on someone you love, someone you don't know at all, someone about whom you have conflicted feelings, or even someone for whom you feel antipathy. Often, we are also instructed to direct our feelings of compassion toward ourselves. Students of this type of meditation frequently report that this last step is the hardest. For some of us, it is harder to experience compassionate feelings toward ourselves than toward our worst enemy. If that's the case, it might be extra important to work on this skill.

Generally, if you're an outwardly compassionate person (compassionate toward others), see if you can turn that compassion inward—toward yourself. Ask yourself if you are treating yourself with the same loving-kindness that you would give to another person. And if the answer is no, try to do so. This can be easier said than done, but it's also not impossible.

Self-compassion meditation practices help us recognize what compassion feels like in our minds and bodies and then helps us practice turning those feelings toward ourselves. Some exercises instruct us to say things to ourselves like, "Dara, may you know peace" or "Jamie, may you hold yourself in compassion," addressing yourself with your own name.[1] Through compassion meditation practices, we can evoke the feelings associated with compassion (spaciousness, warmth, softness, light, love, and strength) while thinking of loved ones and then, while in that state, focus that energy on ourselves.

We have suggestions for resources on compassion and self-compassion in the appendix.

WATCHING THE SELF-TALK

As discussed in Chapter 3, automatic thoughts can play a role in how we treat ourselves. Consider some of the harsh language Juan used about himself in the earlier example. Do you have a harsh inner critic? Do you find yourself thinking really negative things about yourself or your actions? For example, some us probably say, "Well, that's dumb" to ourselves on a regular basis. Would you say that to someone else? Probably not. Then don't say it to yourself! I (Dara) apparently said some things like this out loud in the past because

---

[1]You may notice that some practices, on the other hand, use the first person: "May I know peace." Try different variations and see what feels more comfortable and impactful for you.

my grandmother used to say, "Hey! Don't talk like that about my granddaughter!" You have our permission to modify this thought to suit your circumstances: When you find yourself saying something self-deprecating, feel free to imagine us (Dara and Jamie) saying, "Hey! Don't talk like that about our reader!"

So, what's the antidote here? Well, we'd recommend reminding yourself (as an alternative thought or a response to your negative automatic thought) that you are human. Humans make mistakes. I (Jamie) practice this with my own children by making a game out of it, asking my kids after school, "Who made a mistake today?" I always raise my hand and share some area of my life in which I made a mistake. I then discuss what happened and what it felt like. My family then celebrates these mistakes together. No one has 100% good ideas. Perhaps it would help to start with just minor revisions to the negative self-talk. If you find yourself calling yourself stupid or calling one of your ideas dumb, maybe try to rewrite that thought to: "Hmm. That might not be the best idea I ever had. . . ."

Remember some of the thoughts that Juan was having about himself. He thought he should be braver in approaching his family about his sexual orientation. What evidence does he have that he isn't brave? He has put himself out there in the activist group and in activities on campus in ways that many people would never consider doing. Most people would probably consider that to be pretty brave! He is concerned about the consequences of sharing his sexual orientation with his family because he knows they believe that homosexuality is not acceptable. His concerns that he may be rejected by them are valid, given their views, and it makes sense that he would be hesitant to come out to them. If Juan could reframe the situation and think about it from this perspective, perhaps he could adjust his self-talk to be something like, "I really want to find a way to come out to my family. It makes sense that I'm hesitant, given their views, but maybe there's a way to do this." This more understanding perspective might allow Juan to engage in some helpful reflection or conversations about whether (or when) he wants to come out to his family, rather than making him feel ashamed for not having done so yet.

NATURE

Think about a time when you went for a walk in nature. Perhaps your intention was to get some exercise and enjoy the nice day. On your return, you felt a sense of peace and calm that you hadn't expected. A lot of research suggests that being in nature is good for our well-being and health. There is even a term for spending time in nature to reap mental health benefits: *shinrin-yoku*, or *forest bathing*.

Forest bathing is about more than just being in nature. Forest bathing is also about being mindfully present in nature and absorbing all of the sensations that are present in your experience. What sounds do you hear in the forest? What are you smelling as you walk along the trail? What are you seeing? It's about being present in the moment and using your senses to experience all that surrounds you. It's about letting your senses explore and indulge in all of nature's beauty.

Perhaps you are thinking, "There really aren't any forests near me. This doesn't apply to me; I live in the city." A walk in a public park or even down your own street can allow some engagement with nature. I (Jamie) find even a small dose of nature can help me start the day better, such as sitting on my deck and listening to birds and watching the trees in the morning (instead of being glued to my phone). It can be done in the sun, rain, or snow and at any time of year. It's about allowing your senses to explore nature, whether in a large landscape or a small one.

Forest bathing has a lot of health benefits. Studies in Japan have found that anger, anxiety, fatigue, and depression decrease after forest bathing, and positive emotions like vigor increase. Stress hormones and blood pressure are shown to decrease after engaging in forest bathing. Research has also found increases in immune function after forest bathing. Overall, the health benefits and the subjective experience of feeling better are even more reasons to use nature as a way to take care of yourself.

Consider spending time in nature during your downtime. This is a low-cost way to use the beauty of our planet to recharge our own batteries. Look for ways to spend time closer to trees, flowers, and greenery. Be sure to engage your senses when you are in this setting, and keep your phone at home or in the car. It's important to disconnect when engaging in this experience so that you can be more present.

SELF-SOOTHING

Many of us heard of the term "self-soothing" when we had infants. The goal is to get them to transition from having to depend on adults to soothe them to being able to do it themselves. It's about helping the baby find a way to calm themselves down so they can gain more independence, especially at night. Some babies find this easier than others. You can usually tell which ones when you look at the level of exhaustion on the faces of the parents.

Self-soothing techniques are mostly physical activities that we engage in to feel better or calmer, or to feel more pleasure and relaxation. However, from an evolutionary standpoint, *self-soothing* is really about activating the parasympathetic nervous system (think: opposite of fight-or-flight) to either calm yourself when you are already stressed or to prevent the fight-or-flight response from happening. Self-soothing relates to the concept of self-compassion in that the goal is to comfort, nurture, and be kind to yourself. If you face many of the world's injustices or horrors every day, self-soothing skills are likely lifelines to help yourself recoup.

These techniques involve each of the five senses: (a) vision, (b) hearing, (c) smell, (d) taste, and (e) touch. For instance, in terms of vision, you can look at the stars or moon at night. Go for a walk in the park or take a scenic hike. Light a candle in the room and watch the flame. Look at a colorful flower or watch the sun rise or set. The idea is to find beauty in your visual field and use this as a way to calm yourself and find pleasure.

Self-soothing using hearing involves finding sounds or music that can help you with relaxing and finding contentment. It could be listening to soothing music or your favorite songs, or to the sounds of nature like waves, birds, rainfall, and so on. If you play an instrument or want to learn how, the sounds from engaging in this task can be soothing. You might notice that you seek out different sounds or different types of music when you're in different moods. For example, your favorite disco (or Nu-disco) song may not be exactly what you want to listen to at the end of a long day of work.

In terms of self-soothing techniques related to the sense of smell, you can use scents as a way to comfort or nurture yourself. As with the other senses, this type of self-soothing could involve smells in nature, such as smelling fresh pine or flowers. It can also involve opening a window and smelling the air. Take a lighted candle and smell its aroma. You may also want to mindfully smell particular foods, such as spices, coffee, or popcorn.

Self-soothing with taste may involve using flavors from food or having soothing drinks, such as tea or hot chocolate, to comfort yourself. Tasting can also involve eating a favorite childhood food or dessert or a gum that is flavorful.

You can use the sense of touch to provide kindness or comfort to yourself. You may do this by taking a long, hot bath; putting clean sheets on your bed; or getting a massage or practicing self-massage. We often find this comfort in a cozy, warm, or soft blanket. Putting lotion on your body or sinking into a comfortable couch are other examples. I (Dara) have discovered recently that I feel a lot better when wearing comfortable clothing (think: t-shirts and yoga pants or t-shirts and yoga pants that are masquerading as dressy/work-appropriate clothes). Remember that your clothes are touching you all day; what feels mildly uncomfortable in the morning may be pretty annoying by the end of the day. Soothing touch is also a part of some self-compassion practices: You might be asked to put your hand on your heart or give yourself a hug. See which of these bring you comfort. Some people find water to be particularly soothing in its contact with your body. A bath or even a swim might be relaxing or soothing.

HOBBIES

What is a hobby? Some of you reading this may be asking yourself that question. If you are engaged in a lot of work to change the world, you may not have much time for hobbies. You may have memories of doing activities considered hobbies when you were younger and had more time. However, it isn't too late for you to either pick up a hobby that you put down years ago or start something new.

Hobbies are things that you enjoy doing that are leisure and not related to work. While some hobbies can be expensive, others can be almost free, other than the time spent doing them. For instance, crafts, woodworking, sewing, and arts are considered hobbies for many. If you enjoy drawing, painting, knitting, or crocheting (and don't do it for a living!), you have a hobby. Some people collect things as a hobby. Remember that stamp or rock collection you had as a child? Yep, that is a hobby. Gardening, playing music, and reading are other hobbies.

You may be wondering why you should make time for a hobby. Perhaps the idea of doing so feels self-indulgent to you. Like all of the other nourishing activities described in this chapter, hobbies are a form of self-care. Having several different hobbies helps us get our mind off of the stress of life and allows us to use our creativity and minds in different ways, challenging and distracting us (in good ways). Finding new hobbies or practicing old ones may provide a mood boost. Because our lives are always changing, it's important to be able to find this joy in different places.

Hobbies, like other activities, such as helping others, shopping, eating a good meal, or having sex, give our brain a little release or boost of dopamine. Having hobbies allows us to get a break from our work and do something else that feels good. For instance, I (Jamie) am an avid reader and usually read more than 50 books a year. I read all of these books for free through my library app. Many people have asked me how I do it with two young children, a demanding job, and other obligations. I tell them that I prioritize reading after the children go to bed because it is something I really enjoy doing and look forward to. Every night, I read for about 2 hours. Doing so also relates back to boundaries. I could spend time grading or writing to elected officials, but I purposely set this time aside for myself because I know I am much better at my other work when I do it. I get satisfaction every year when I complete my goal and regular satisfaction from finding a great book to get lost in!

As we work to make a difference in the world, it is important to consider other areas of our lives that bring satisfaction, too. Hobbies can provide us a respite from our work and give us a chance to find joy from other places. You may also find that in the process of expanding your horizons, you find new and exciting ways to approach your work. Using different areas of our brains by engaging in activities often helps give the other areas a boost, too!

DOING LESS

Yes, that's what we said. Do less than you are currently doing. Sometimes self-care involves doing more "nothing." Some readers may find this to be strange advice, especially if you are trying to use this book to get ready to do more. However, sometimes doing nothing or just focusing on what you need to do for you is exactly what you need. The Dutch have a word for this—*niksen*—which involves just being without any other purpose. Yes, you may think you are not accomplishing as much. However, is doing less really not accomplishing anything? Let's take a look.

We all hit a wall or a time when we realize what we are doing to change the world doesn't seem effective. It could be we are just tired, or maybe it's the dead of winter and it doesn't feel like there is good work to be done. It may also be that our heart isn't in it. We just don't feel the drive or desire to go to our volunteer position. We may find our mood becoming more negative or pessimistic. We could be acting not like ourselves. It is important during these times to give ourselves a break and to rest to recharge our batteries.

Doing nothing may be an act of self-compassion—of being kind to ourselves. We only have so much life in our proverbial batteries, and sometimes when we are not getting them recharged, we need to take time out. Perhaps these breaks consist of relaxing at home and spending time with loved ones (recall the many benefits of social support discussed in Chapter 4).

European American culture emphasizes doing, achieving, and obtaining success, as is seen in the way we work and in our inability to fully relax during breaks and vacations (as compared with many other cultures—perhaps, in part, because our vacations are often shorter). Often our work doesn't end at 5 p.m., and it's hard for many people to keep work from spilling over into their homelife. Kids are often overscheduled themselves, with parents so anxious about their success that they sign them up for too many activities. But research suggests that slowing down is associated with a host of health benefits from decreased anxiety to improved immune function, to increased capacity for creative ideas.

You only get one life, and even if you have a strong desire to make your mark by working on helping others or a cause, it's still okay—even important—to give yourself permission to take a break every so often. You need to make sure you take care of yourself and prioritize doing less. Make sure you take your vacations—and at least some vacations that are low key—so you don't come home feeling like you need a vacation from your vacation.

SEEKING TREATMENT

Before we (temporarily) leave the topic of getting the care you need, let's talk about therapy. How do you know when the things you can do on your own may not be enough? When is it time to seek help?

Psychologists (and the medical community) define psychological experiences as *disorders* if they involve distress or impairment. *Distress* refers to whether the symptoms or other experiences are upsetting to you. For example, if you've been sleeping less recently and it's really bothering you, we would say that the sleep disturbance is causing distress. *Impairment* refers to interference with your functioning in one or more life domains. Perhaps that lack of sleep makes it hard for you to focus at work, and your work is suffering. Or maybe your grades are slipping. Impairment can occur in your personal or home life, too. Perhaps you are withdrawing from your friends or are unable to take care of yourself, your kids, or others who depend on you.

Suppose one or more of these forms of distress or impairment is resonating with you. What now? How do you go about finding a (good) therapist? Well, the kind of strategies you're reading about in this book are mostly based in cognitive behavior therapy (CBT), which is the kind of therapy that both of us practice. If you like this present-focused, practical approach, you might want to seek something similar in treatment. (Don't think that if reading this book "didn't work," then CBT isn't for you. Having a therapist to guide you through treatment, help you select the most useful strategies, and help you implement them effectively is a whole other thing from reading a book.) The professional organization the Association for Behavioral and Cognitive Therapies has a clinician directory that might help you identify a CBT practitioner. You can also learn a bit about potential therapists via *Psychology Today*, a popular clinician directory in the United States (there are also others, like Mental Health Match). You might also ask your internist or family doctor for a recommendation.

We encourage you to ask the therapist how they approach treatment (or you could ask what their "theoretical orientation" is), but that is just one component of the "match" you might be seeking with a therapist. You might ask if they offer a free phone consult to get a feel for them—and you might do this with two to three therapists before starting therapy with one. Once you do start, reevaluate after three or so sessions. If you feel like it might not be a good fit, you can certainly raise your concerns with your therapist, and don't hesitate to switch if you need to. It can be really hard to shop around for a therapist, especially when you're already struggling, but you're investing a lot of time and energy in the therapy process (and possibly money as well), so you want to make sure you're getting as much benefit out of it as you can.

Let's come back to Luke. After continuing to experience emotional challenges at work and with respect to buying a house, Luke decided it was time to seek the help of a therapist. He mentioned to a friend that he was feeling hopeless and that sometimes, no matter how hard he tries, he sees no change. He has been spending time in nature and meditating, but neither of those activities is helping like they have in the past. His friend suggested finding a therapist and commented that Luke may be experiencing depression. While Luke is a bit intimidated about psychotherapy because he has never needed it before and doesn't know what to expect, he does realize that his current feelings are affecting his ability to concentrate at work and his desire to socialize. After a few months of therapy, he recognizes that you don't have to be "crazy" to need help and that he has learned some great cognitive and behavioral strategies to use daily to stay on track, even during the more bumpy or rough periods of life.

BOTTOM LINE

Often, people who are busy taking care of others and of the world don't take great care of themselves. Sometimes we don't prioritize ourselves and our own needs as much as we prioritize others' needs. Sometimes we don't even notice our own needs or know how to respond to them. We may have coping strategies that work well for a time, and then, for whatever reason, they no longer seem a sufficient match for the stressors in our lives.

It's important to remain committed to self-care and to make efforts for it to evolve over time. Remember, too, that many stressors are related to systemic problems. We are not advocating self-care instead of addressing those systemic problems. Rather, we are suggesting that perhaps self-care might help us to stay healthier while addressing them and will allow us to keep the work going.

CHAPTER 9

MAINTAINING MOTIVATION AND AVOIDING BURNOUT

Remember this, however, in the darkest moments, when the work doesn't seem worth it, and change seems just out of reach: out of our willingness to push through comes a tremendous power. . . . So use it.

—Stacey Abrams (2018, p. 206)

On your journey to make a difference in the world, you will likely encounter periods when you feel utterly exhausted. It may be that you feel worn out; very tired; and perhaps even sad, frustrated, and blah. In any of the work that we do in our lives, we may encounter *burnout*, an experience of physical and psychological exhaustion from overwork. Burnout is more likely to happen when we feel a lack of control in a situation and when the demands on us are many. In our efforts to make a difference in the world, whether it's trying to change the trajectory of a child's life or tackling climate change, we may hit a wall and we feel like we have no control—like no amount of effort can succeed in the face of the forces working against us.

LUCIANA'S STORY

Consider the case of Luciana, a 42-year-old, biracial, cisgender gay woman and nutritionist who is an advocate of healthy lunches in schools. As a resident of an inner-city neighborhood, she saw how living in a food desert affected her neighbors and their children. She spent the past few years working with the city council to transform empty lots into urban farm spaces. She also worked with community organizations to help provide the people power needed to transform the land to a beautiful garden, where space was allocated to grow different vegetables and fruits that families in the area would then enjoy.

Almost 2 years to the day that the garden opened, Luciana awoke to a phone call from the police. The transformative space that she had spent so much energy and time on had been destroyed in hours by people who tore out the plants, destroyed the garden boxes, and cut all of the hoses. Luciana was devastated. She found she was depleted of motivation and felt helpless in terms of what to do next. She asked one of the community organizers to take the lead on next steps because she simply could not find the energy to face the destruction.

Motivation can wax and wane for a variety of reasons. It could be something like what Luciana experienced—your hard work is destroyed in an instant—or just that the continuous journey of trying to make a change and hitting brick wall after brick wall takes a toll, and it's hard to go on—an experience we might call burnout. We come back to the topic of burnout at the end of this chapter. But first, how do we get to this point? How do we go from feeling inspired and driven in our work to this place where motivation is hard to find?

Motivation stems from intrinsic (internal) and extrinsic (external) factors. For instance, you might have noticed that you are motivated to engage in behaviors because you enjoy the experience (*intrinsic*). Perhaps you are driven to help those who have been exposed to more harm than you because you feel a responsibility to give back. *Extrinsic* motivators include getting paid, opportunities for promotion, or positive feedback from others. Take a moment to think about what motivates you. Where does the motivation for your work come from? What drives you? There's likely not one answer to this question. We may have different motivations for different activities or multiple motivations for each activity, and our motivations may change over time. Perhaps you originally sought your job because you were inspired by the work, but now you stay because you have a family to support.

As you may have noticed, the intrinsic motivators often seem more satisfying than the extrinsic motivators. Indeed, intrinsic motivators tend to "work" better than extrinsic ones, for the most part, leaving us feeling more satisfied and fulfilled and also leading to our wanting to continue the work. On the other hand, money is a pretty powerful motivator, too!

Motivation often precedes behavior. In other words, if we lack motivation to do something, we are less likely to engage in that behavior. A model called the transtheoretical or stages of change model, summarized in Figure 9.1, shows how some behaviors are initiated and maintained. The general idea is that motivation is not

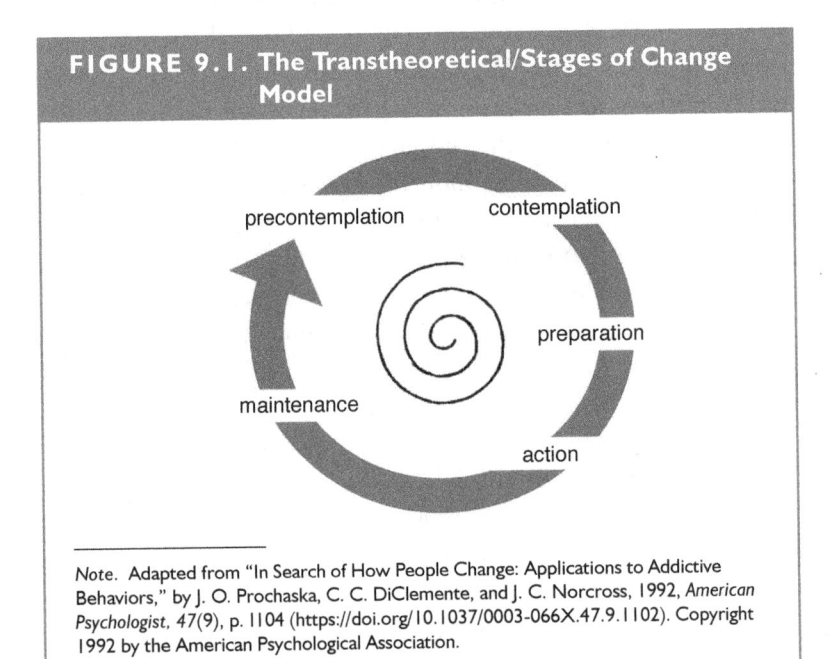

FIGURE 9.1. The Transtheoretical/Stages of Change Model

Note. Adapted from "In Search of How People Change: Applications to Addictive Behaviors," by J. O. Prochaska, C. C. DiClemente, and J. C. Norcross, 1992, *American Psychologist, 47*(9), p. 1104 (https://doi.org/10.1037/0003-066X.47.9.1102). Copyright 1992 by the American Psychological Association.

an all-or-none proposition. We may feel ambivalent about a decision or a behavior, simultaneously both wanting and not wanting to do it. We can often see pros and cons. However, according to the model, our motivation to do something (or to stop doing something) can build over time until the pros outweigh the cons, and we take action.

According to this model, people start the process in the pre-contemplation stage. *Precontemplation* is what we often refer to as denial—the person is not thinking about making a change at all. They don't see a need. If the person does start to consider a given behavior—say, attending local Rotary Club meetings—they then move to the contemplation stage. In the *contemplation* stage, the person is thinking about doing something but with consider-able ambivalence. Perhaps they have a friend who has invited them to go to the meetings. On the one hand, they see how much good the Rotary Club does in the community, and they think they would enjoy socializing with like-minded people. However, evenings are their time with their children, and they don't want to sacrifice that. Given this ambivalence, they haven't yet attended a meeting.

The next stage in the model is *preparation*. This is when an individual begins to prepare to make a change (i.e., take steps toward making that change even though they haven't really made it yet). For instance, in the Rotary Club example, perhaps you talk with your partner about the possibility of going to a meeting, maybe you pick a date to go, or you tell your friend that you will go with them next time. You could even put the address in your GPS and tell your family you are going to go. You haven't actually gone yet, but you are getting ready to in concrete ways.

The next stage is the *action* stage at which we actually begin engaging in the behavior. This is when you are going to the Rotary Club meeting. *Action* means that the desired behavior is happening. You went to your first Rotary Club meeting and are continuing to attend. You are actively engaging in the behavior.

As many of us know, getting started can often be easier than keeping up a behavior or establishing a habit. That is what the *maintenance* stage is about. You have reached this stage when you have been engaging in this behavior for 6 months or more and are perhaps at a point at which you begin to get other people to go to the meeting. You may bring a friend or two and encourage them to join, and you keep going yourself. Maybe you have become such a regular that they have you in charge of the check-ins at the beginning of the meeting or have you introduce the speakers.

The spiral in the middle of the illustration is a reminder that we may not move through these stages in order. We don't always go straight from action to maintenance, for instance; we may end up back in contemplation again, perhaps going through action again and then to maintenance. For example, perhaps you go to meetings for a few months but then a conflict arises, and you miss one. The following week you skip another, and pretty soon you stop going altogether. You may go back to the precontemplation stage at which you aren't considering going back to the meetings, and go back through this cycle. The spiral design also reminds us, though, that we learn something each time we revisit a stage that may contribute toward our long-term success.

You may be asking why you need to know this. It's helpful to understand some of the theories as to why we engage in behaviors—or don't—so that we can do things to help ourselves along the way. Knowing that motivation is fluid, we can use tools to help us enhance motivation when it is lacking and get ourselves back on the path toward our valued directions.

MOTIVATIONAL INTERVIEWING

If you find your motivation to be lacking, but you want to kick it into gear, you can do a few things to help yourself. Motivational interviewing (MI), mentioned briefly in Chapter 5, is a clinical tool developed by William Miller and Stephen Rollnick (2013) to help individuals who struggle with substance use problems address their ambivalence about quitting. It's not just for addictions, though; it's helpful in moving from one stage to the next of the stages of change model, with respect to a variety of life changes. Earlier in the book, we discussed some active listening skills that come from MI. These are generally skills used in a conversation in which the person trained in MI is trying to help someone else resolve ambivalence or otherwise progress through the stages. We think some of the principles can be helpful in dealing with the ebbs and flows of our own motivation as well.

MI is not interviewing as we tend to think of interviewing; rather, it's a conversation or counseling style, and it includes a series of techniques that can be beneficial for you as you try to change a behavior. MI works best for someone who is experiencing ambivalence about a behavior change—someone who sees benefits of making a change but also struggles with the negative consequences of doing it. The ambivalence keeps them in the same spot, not engaging in the "desired" behavior. There may be varying degrees of ambivalence throughout the different stages, although the contemplation stage is the one most characterized by ambivalence.

How do we then deal with this ambivalence to make a positive change? First, it's important to think about what your goal state is. Take out a sheet of paper or an electronic device and write down what it is you want your life to look like in terms of this behavior (or behaviors). Be specific and write about this vision in the present tense. What activities are you engaging in? How are you feeling? What is your relationship with others like? What is a typical day like for you? The more details, the better. Take your time with this.

After you are finished describing your goal state, describe what your life is like now. Go into detail about what your day is like. What activities are you engaging in? How do you feel when engaging in them? How is this different from where you want to be?

Let's consider Luke, who has been struggling with mixed feelings about his job, as described in Chapter 1. This exercise would be useful in his situation as he compares potentially looking for a new job to staying in his current position. If you find yourself in a situation similar to his, try this exercise. While we often "know" what we want and that we are unhappy with what we are doing, taking the time to describe and experience these feelings and situations goes a long way to helping with change.

The purpose of this activity is for you to see a discrepancy between what you are doing and your goal state (you may remember we did a similar exercise earlier, in Chapter 2, with respect to aligning our daily lives with our values). The hope is that by doing this exercise, you start to feel a bit uncomfortable. That's right—we are purposefully making you feel anxious and uncomfortable about your life. Why? Well, this is where cognitive dissonance comes in. *Cognitive dissonance* occurs when we hold inconsistent beliefs about something, or we believe one thing and are engaging in a behavior that is not aligned with our beliefs. This discrepancy creates discomfort and can leave us feeling anxious, sad, shameful, or distressed. According to cognitive dissonance theory, the dissonance leads us to change one of two things: We either change our behavior to be consistent with our beliefs, or we change our beliefs to be consistent with our behavior.

Let's consider a situation affecting the uncle of Angelique, the woman we met in Chapter 6 (she's Marcella's friend). Uncle Harold, a 58-year-old, Caribbean American, cisgender man, has been experiencing health problems. After taking a hard fall at home, he is in a rehabilitation center trying to get better so he can go home. It's likely he will need hip surgery in the next few years. During his time in rehab, he finds out that he is losing his health insurance. He has always been opposed to the idea of universal or government health care because he feels no one should get anything for free. Unfortunately, he now finds himself in a situation in which he may need to rely on programs like Medicaid to help with his own health problems.

In Harold's situation, if he decides to apply for Medicaid to help with his health care, he will likely experience some discomfort with that decision, given his beliefs about universal or subsidized health care. He clearly needs help with his medical costs, so it's likely that he will move forward with Medicaid. How, then, does this affect his beliefs? It's likely that Harold will have to modify his beliefs in some way to justify using a program that he has always viewed so negatively. He may not necessarily move to the pro-universal health care camp (although he might). However, he could adopt a more moderate attitude toward these programs and realize that they are needed in some situations and maybe aren't as bad as he had thought.

By engaging in the writing activity described earlier, to highlight discrepancies, you may find that you elicit your own cognitive dissonance and feel like you need to do something to resolve it. It may still take some time to make a change, but you are getting closer. Remember: Motivation is not binary—that is, it's not typically the case that we are either motivated or not. It's more often the case that we are *somewhat* motivated, and our motivation may grow over time. Nothing is gained by berating ourselves for not having made the change yet. Instead, focus on the discrepancy between your current state and your goal state as well as on how you can resolve that discrepancy. MI focuses on rolling with resistance and providing acceptance and compassion to the person trying to make a change (in this instance, you!).

Another tool from MI is called *decisional balance*, a process of examining the advantages and disadvantages of changing our behavior. Perhaps you've done this for other behaviors or for important decisions. The process is a bit different in MI, though, from how pros and cons lists typically work.

In MI, we create a pros and cons grid to go through a list of the benefits (pros) of engaging in a behavior and the negative consequences (cons) of doing so. Importantly, we then make a list of the pros and cons of *not* engaging in the behavior, too. We end up with a grid like the one shown in Table 9.1.

This may feel a little redundant, but it turns out that we tend to generate different things in each quadrant. For example, under "Disadvantages of the new behavior" (the cons) in the table for the Rotary Club example, we might list: "I might not know anyone except my friend, so I'll feel uncomfortable." But, under "Advantages

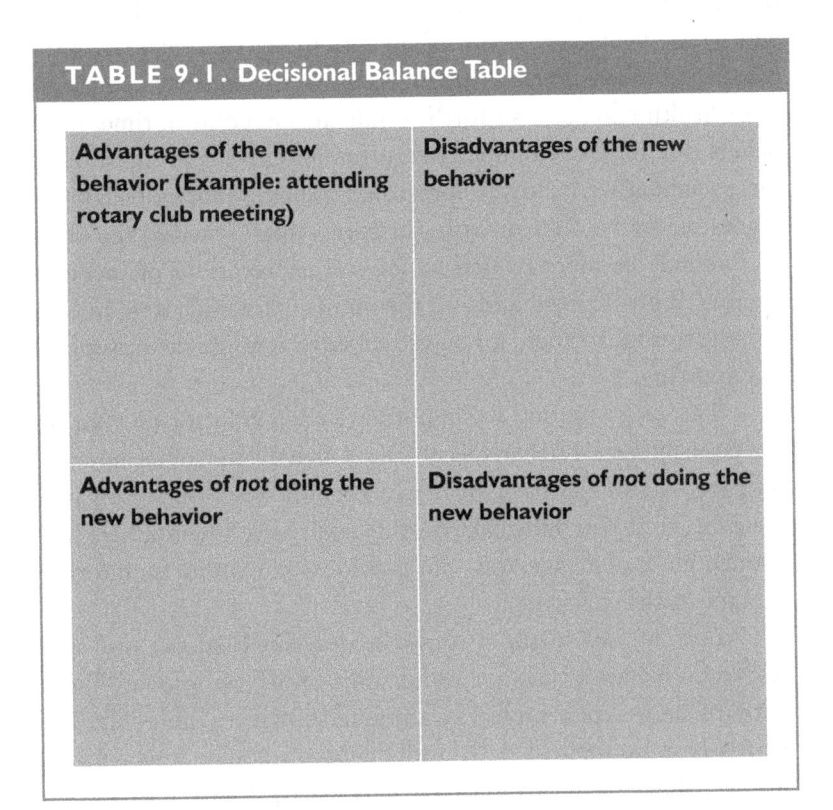

TABLE 9.1. Decisional Balance Table

Advantages of the new behavior (Example: attending rotary club meeting)	Disadvantages of the new behavior
Advantages of *not* doing the new behavior	Disadvantages of *not* doing the new behavior

of *not* doing the new behavior" (which you might think was the other side of the same coin), what might come to mind first might be: "Get to stay home with my kids."

In some versions of the decisional balance exercise, people then assign a "weight" to each of these factors, reflecting how important each of them is, on a scale from 1 (*slightly important*) to 4 (*extremely important*). For instance, if we ask Harold (from the earlier example) to list the pros for applying for Medicaid, he might come up with a list that includes having health care, not going bankrupt, and keeping his house. Perhaps most of those things would rate pretty high. If we ask him to identify the cons of getting Medicaid, he may come up with things that relate to being a drain on the system, relying on the government for help, getting poor health care, and so forth. While at one point in time, these beliefs may have been important, given his current circumstances, these might now rate lower. Sometimes the items that we weight the highest are most aligned with our core values, whereas the other factors may be more related to societal expectations or inconveniences. When Harold adds up the numbers for each item in each cell, the reasons to apply for Medicaid may outweigh the reasons for not applying.

This task of rating the importance of each factor on your list can be an important step in this process. Often the sum of the numbers on each side of the pro/con list can reflect where a person is in the process. If you find that you still don't have the numbers high enough make a change, that can provide you with useful information for further reflection.

Luke himself might also use the decisional balance tool with respect to his dissatisfaction about some of his job responsibilities. Perhaps he makes a table like the one shown in Table 9.2. This matrix is an example of an MI tool that we can pull out when we're feeling conflicted about things. We're not suggesting that we have to

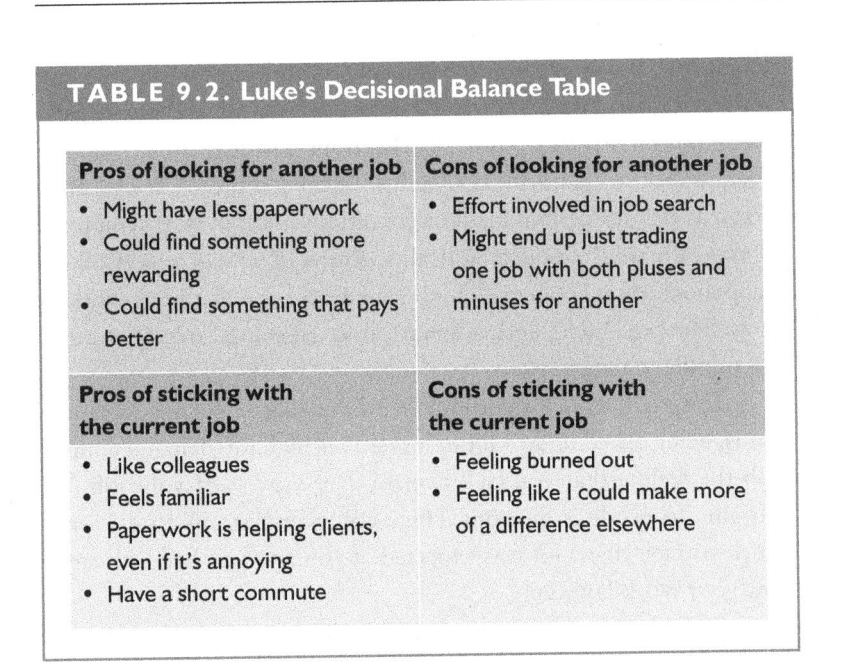

TABLE 9.2. Luke's Decisional Balance Table

Pros of looking for another job	Cons of looking for another job
• Might have less paperwork • Could find something more rewarding • Could find something that pays better	• Effort involved in job search • Might end up just trading one job with both pluses and minuses for another

Pros of sticking with the current job	Cons of sticking with the current job
• Like colleagues • Feels familiar • Paperwork is helping clients, even if it's annoying • Have a short commute	• Feeling burned out • Feeling like I could make more of a difference elsewhere

do what the table suggests, but completing the exercise can lead to important insights.

BURNOUT

The ideas we've described might help you get ready to take steps to do something new. What about when you're doing something important that used to seem meaningful, but you've lost motivation? If this is a volunteer activity, you might be able to just step out for a bit. Alternatively, you could try to find a way to reconnect with your drive and stay involved. And what about when you feel this way about your job? You might be experiencing burnout.

The World Health Organization now recognizes burnout as an "occupational phenomenon"—it's not a psychological disorder, but it is real. Burnout can come from any of the work we do, whether it is service, household, or occupational. It can have consequences both emotionally and physically. Burnout can lead to depression, anger, higher stress hormones, and physical symptoms. It can put a person at risk for certain medical conditions and physical symptoms. We typically think of burnout in the context of jobs or careers. Some occupations are at greater risk for burnout, such as health care workers, service workers, firefighters, administrative assistants, factory workers, and middle managers.

The risk factors for burnout include having a high job demand— that is, being asked to do a lot of tasks. This high job demand coupled with the feeling that you lack control over aspects of your job may combine to produce burnout. Have you ever been in a position in which you felt that a lot was expected of you, but you had little say in how your workday went?

Consider someone who works in the restaurant business as a server, as both of us have done. As a server, you have to quickly greet and fill orders for the patrons (high job demand) but have little to no say in how quickly the kitchen can fill orders (low control). Another example is a social worker who helps people get through homelessness and obtain services After the economy takes a downward turn, the social worker may feel overwhelmed by the number of individuals they are serving and the limitations of the resources available. When there are limited resources, but the problem is intensifying, feelings of helplessness and hopelessness can arise, which can affect the risk of burnout.

It turns out that doctors are also at high risk of burnout in part because of the serious consequences of their work and partly because they don't have control over their days either; someone else typically schedules their appointments. Burnout among medical workers increased during the height of the coronavirus (COVID-19) pandemic, when not only did the amount and demands of their work increase, but the resources (staff and hospital beds) became depleted, leading many people to feel things were even more out of their control.

Other factors that can affect job-related stress include ambiguity in one's role at their job. For instance, perhaps it's not clear what you are supposed to be doing or what the expectations are. Is there a lot of conflict or drama in your workplace? This can be another source of stress that can lead to burnout. Inequities at work and inadequate career advancement are also factors.

Some of these risk factors may affect your work to make a difference in the world, and they may affect you in other ways, too. If you spend your free time trying to enhance and protect wildlife sanctuaries in your area, but your day job is as an emergency room nurse, you may feel the effects of burnout from your daytime job, which may, in turn, affect your motivation for your environmental work. It may also start to affect other aspects of your life: your relationships, family, health, and leisure.

Burnout can appear in many different ways. In political campaigns, we see fluctuations in mental and physical exhaustion across the election cycle. If you have worked on a campaign, you will know the drill: For a November election in the United States, activities—events, fundraisers, and so on—may start to pick up in the spring and summer and become utterly chaotic in the fall leading up to an election. Motivation is high because there is a deadline. After the election, it is easy for motivation to decrease and sometimes become nonexistent. People sometimes describe feeling a "crash" after big events they have been working toward for a long time.

What are signs of burnout? It can appear as exhaustion or fatigue. It can also lead to a lack of productivity at work or in other areas of life. You may find it difficult to get started at your work and have trouble focusing or paying attention. Having a cynical or critical attitude toward your work or coworkers is another sign. You may find yourself irritable, impatient, or angry with the people you interact with through work. This irritability may even carry over to your loved ones or friends. Your patience may be thin, and you may find that you are not coping well with everyday stressors. Individuals can experience despair or sadness. Some people may not get the same satisfaction from their work as they previously did. Physical symptoms, such as stomach problems, increased and unexplained headaches, or sleep disturbance, can also occur. Some people experience an increase in using food or substances to cope with these feelings, which can lead to weight gain or problematic substance use.

What can help with burnout? Maintaining a good work–life balance seems to help, although achieving this balance is an ongoing challenge for many. Having a number of positive and restorative experiences with family or friends or participating in enjoyable activities may help counteract the experience of burnout. It's important not to work all the time but to truly enjoy leisure time and rest. Remember also, as mentioned in Chapter 8, that compassion meditation can help with burnout. Perhaps you can use some of your leisure time to practice compassion or self-compassion.

Having friends and family who provide social support can also help. Talking through your stressors or venting to others is a great way to relieve the burden of stress and increase positive emotions. Perhaps you notice a boost in your mood after a night with friends or neighbors. It could be that talking about the week's stressors with a friend helps to relieve the burden of them.[1] Social support can help you feel like you are not carrying your burdens alone. It could also

---

[1] At the same time, we want to caution against getting caught up in complaining, which can make us ruminate about problems even more and might be counterproductive. Just check in with yourself while having these conversations to see what impact they are having on your mood. And, if you need to, feel free to say explicitly, "Hey, you know? Let's stop talking shop. I'm not sure this is helping."

be that having fun and laughing gets your mind off of the problem. Laughter is great medicine for our souls! Interestingly, not only does social support help with burnout, research finds that it is a predictor of positive health outcomes and longevity.

Don't forget to celebrate the successes you do have, and remember that they might not all look like achieving your goal (some may represent small steps toward a long-term goal). Recall positive reinforcement? It applies here, too. We not only need positive things to happen to stay motivated, but we also need to recognize them as positive. Maybe the city considers your grant but does not approve it. Celebrate that you submitted it and that it was considered. These pauses to celebrate successes are important for motivation and to keep our momentum going.

While it may seem silly to celebrate small things like organizing a rally or helping an elder connect with needed services, each small wave we create has the potential to create other waves. We may not always know how big this success really was; the ripple effect could be large (as an analogy, think about how paying for coffee for the person behind you in the drive-through may impact their day and the days of those they encounter). Pause and reflect after your work (big or small), and remember that putting the positive energy for change into the world is a success in its own right. Stacey Abrams, whose words are quoted at the start of this chapter, has also said, "I learned long ago that winning doesn't always mean you get the prize. Sometimes you get progress, and that counts" (Abrams, 2020, p. 6).

We often want to immediately see the results of the work that we do. However, with some work (in fact, maybe a lot of it), we may never truly see the fruits of our labor. It may be that our work helps people we may never meet. Consider the work of the Cystic Fibrosis Foundation, a nonprofit organization that seeks to increase both the life span and quality of life of patients with cystic fibrosis (CF). Founded in 1955 by a group of concerned parents who were dedicated to saving the lives of their children, the foundation has provided money for research on new drugs to help treat CF. While the original founders of the organization did not see their own children benefit from these new drugs, the lifespan of children with CF has quadrupled from an average age of 10 years in 1962 to the age of 44 in 2020—all thanks to parents who worked so hard, even after having lost their own children.

RIDING THE WAVES OF MOTIVATION

Maintaining motivation can be difficult, especially when you are working against systems that aren't easily changed or that take a long time to show results. You may find that, at times, you feel like giving up. It's important to remember that these are normal experiences, thoughts, and feelings to have. Just because you have the thought of quitting or that you are ineffective does not mean you are; it just means that you had a thought (remember cognitive defusion?). Having competing demands or other priorities can make maintaining motivation even more difficult. It is okay to allow yourself to take a break to rejuvenate yourself or to take on a less demanding task so that you still feel like you are contributing but with less demand placed on you.

Motivation can also come in waves. If you are experiencing a burst of motivational energy, you may want to ride the wave and take advantage of it. It may be short-lived, so using that time to accomplish more is helpful, if you can do it. Doing so can not only accomplish a few things on your list (e.g., making calls to local constituents on behalf of a school board candidate) and help you reach your long-term goal (e.g., getting someone elected), but it can also lead to a sense of accomplishment and boost your confidence in your ability to get things done, which may make it easier to engage in this behavior in the future. I (Jamie) find that my motivation varies depending on the time of day (mornings tend to be associated with higher levels of motivation) and physical activity. After exercising, I find that my mind tends to be more focused. If I want to be productive, I also turn off my phone and minimize email and other distractors on my computer so I can make the most of this time. See if you notice patterns in your own motivation, productivity, and focus. Perhaps you can rearrange some of your tasks to work with those patterns.

It's also important to know when low motivation is related to something more serious like major depressive disorder, which shares some features with burnout. Major depression is a common psychological disorder, and low motivation is often a symptom along with sadness, a lack of interest in things that you once found enjoyable, fatigue, sleep disturbance, and difficulty concentrating, to name a few. If you are experiencing these symptoms for longer than 2 weeks (most of the day, nearly every day), it's important to reach out for help. These symptoms can also be accompanied by negative thoughts about yourself and sometimes suicidal ideation. Although it is not always clear how to differentiate burnout from depression, if you find that these symptoms are affecting your day-to-day life and ability to function, it is a good idea to talk to your physician (also see Chapter 8 for the discussion about seeking psychotherapy).

BOTTOM LINE

Like so many things in life, motivation is ever changing: At one point in time, we may find ourselves with an abundance of energy to make a difference, and, at other times, that energy may dwindle. Perhaps life has handed you problems that make it difficult to focus on your change-work. That does not mean you have to abandon it forever. Come back to this chapter when you find yourself in a slump or need some tools to get through a tough period. Remember: Change is constant, and motivation may ebb and flow.

CHAPTER 10

THE LONG TERM: HOW MIGHT YOUR ENGAGEMENT EVOLVE OVER TIME?

It starts from the bottom up, not from the top down. Every bit of progress we've made—starting with the abolition movement, through women's suffrage, through the union movement, through the modern civil rights movement—politicians typically followed, rather than led, in terms of big progress.
—President Barack Obama
(Obama Foundation, 2021, 29:39)

As mentioned at the end of Chapter 9, the one constant in life is, of course, change. Perhaps a change in your life prompted you to rethink how you are making a difference in the world. It could have resulted from politics, a cultural shift, or even a personal tragedy. It could have been what guided your career to help others in the first place or your service work to make a difference.

The drive to make a difference comes from deep within. However, as we discussed in the previous chapter, the energy for this work will wax and wane over time. Our priorities may shift, and life will change. It's helpful to acknowledge that over the life span, events will occur that can trigger changes in our priorities. Consider two individuals we have been following in this book: Luke and Marcella. We don't know what the future will hold for either of them. It's likely that as they age and go through different life stages, they may see changes in what they think is important and what kind of work they want to do to make the world a better place. We may even see them take a break from their social justice commitment for a while as other priorities grab their attention. This chapter is intended to help you ride these waves of motivation and capacity. We want to remind you that any difference you make is worthwhile. We also want to help you consolidate the lessons contained in this book that might be useful to you as you ride those waves.

It makes sense that what we value most changes over the life span. Think about what was important to you in your childhood and adolescence and how that has changed as you have gotten older. In adolescence, often our priorities are social, and our worlds may feel smaller. As we get older and realize the vast nature of our world and the interconnectedness of things and the world around us, we may become more invested in making a difference. For example, I (Jamie) find that thinking about climate change and its effects is less meaningful when I think of my own life but more meaningful when I think of how it will affect my children or grandchildren. Perhaps access to health care isn't that important to you if you have private insurance through your employer, but as soon as you find, say, your parent in a position in which they lose their job at 62 years of age—as well as health care for them and their spouse or partner— it becomes more crucial to you and to them. We expect that our interests in making a difference will change as our lives do.

While shifts in interests and passions may change gradually, there may be times when a shift is more sudden. Remember that all of these changes are okay (refer to Chapter 4 for help when you have difficulty accepting this notion). It's also okay to take a break from one thing to pursue a different interest or to follow a path you discover along the way. Take time during this journey to reflect on the process of what making the world a better place means to you and how the experience of doing this work affects you on a day-to-day basis and in your life as a whole.

Is the work adding to your life in a meaningful way? Has this experience led to more positive energy in your life and a feeling of satisfaction? Perhaps you are having more negative experiences than positive ones because of the work you are doing right now. It's crucial to take the time to process—to explore the feelings more deeply to understand them. You can do this through journaling or by taking notes on what work you are doing, why you are doing it, and how it makes you feel. Just like a gardener who keeps notes on their garden year after year to note soil changes, new plants tried, and so on, note both how the changes in our lives (or in the outside world) impact our work toward change and also how we feel about the work, our motivation, and the satisfaction we get from the work.

Importantly, accept lulls that may occur in your justice work. After having a child or while caring for a sick or dying family member, your action work may have to take a backseat. That is okay. Our own health issues (including mental health) can also affect this work. We need to recognize when our health is suffering from the stress of our social action work and take a break to avoid burnout or other negative outcomes. As in the analogy of the oxygen mask on a plane that we mentioned in Chapter 4, we can't do this work if we aren't well. The analogy of pouring from an empty cup is also a useful one, here: Not only do all humans deserve to have our cups replenished, but we will be far more effective in helping others and changing the world if we do.

Sometimes we may discover that we are in a lull, even though we didn't really mean to be and don't necessarily need to be. Maybe you were sick one week a few weeks ago and so skipped the weekly meeting of your grassroots organization. Then, the following week, you forgot, and before you know it, you discover you haven't been to a meeting in 2 months. Sometimes it can feel hard to step back in after a long break, or you might find yourself having thoughts like, "Well, I guess I didn't manage to keep that going" or "I'm too embarrassed to face the group now." Remember: It is not too late to get back into it! Most likely your friends and fellow activists will be thrilled to see you when you return. Sometimes, if our habits start to drift, we just need to press a "reset button."

Staying engaged at high levels in this work may not be sustainable all the time. Feeling motivated to make a difference but being unable to keep up the same pace as in the past is okay. Engaging and mentoring future generations of advocates and facilitators of change is another phase of this work. It may be that you train others to do this work, and that in and of itself is making a difference—and it may make it easier for you to take a step back, when needed, knowing you are leaving the work in good hands. Teach the lessons you have learned to the next generation. Share your stories. Tell them the tales of your successes. Remember the power of stories from the discussion in Chapter 5? There is a lot to be gained by sharing your story and experience with others. Perhaps you convinced a nonvoter to register to vote or you helped get a bill passed at the state level. Let others carry the torch, and let their energy guide the wave of change. Help them to be the change.

As mentioned throughout this book, the messages that lead us to our advocacy or change work came at different points in our life—some from our parents in childhood or others as a result of events in our own lives or communities. Regardless, as Anne Frank noted (see the Introduction), every person has the opportunity to make change in the world around them. I (Jamie) talk about the power each of my children and students have to facilitate change. In my classes, I cover topics like health disparities and the way that social factors affect stress and health. My students often become frustrated by these discussions because they feel powerless to do anything about the social factors. These are my favorite moments of class: It's when I remind them that they do not have to accept things the way they are. Each one of them has the power to help facilitate change.

While you are now reading the last chapter of this book, please remember that this resource will be here for you along the journey.

We hope that you find this book to be a useful reference that you can come back to from time to time. These chapters can be read and reread in any order and at any time. You may find it helpful to revisit how your values have shifted and changed—perhaps reviewing Chapter 1 could facilitate that process. If you find it difficult to manage your emotions or find that negative thoughts keep sneaking in and affecting your ability to do the work, revisit Chapters 3 and 4. Self-compassion and kindness are essential to being successful at this work and not allowing burnout to overtake you—and they can be hard to maintain. Therefore, you may want to periodically review Chapters 8 and 9. And don't forget the additional resources in the appendix. Maybe you would benefit from taking a deeper dive into some of these topics. We provide guidance on where to go to do that.

We hope that you now see ways that you can use what you know about yourself, your thoughts, your feelings, and your behaviors to keep going in this work. Pausing to reflect—on what's working for us and what's not—can help us make adjustments that can make our work more sustainable. Sometimes negative thoughts get in our way. Sometimes a mismatch between our valued directions and our daily activities can be a sign that we may have drifted in a direction that is less satisfying, and we might want to make some changes. When we find ourselves frustrated with others, we might want to think about how we can be more intentional in our communication to get us closer to our goals.

As we end our journey together, we would like to remind you that others out there want to change the world—just like you. You are never alone. We all came to this work because we saw something that wasn't right and felt the need to do something. While many, many people are troubled by injustices in the world around them, not everyone steps up to the plate to try to make the world better. In any of a number of activities, when you see an injustice or something that does not seem right to you, know that you have the power to make a difference. You are touching lives and making the world a better place. Keep a broad view of what this work means and embrace how it changes over your life. Remember that wisdom comes from age and experience and that we all have ways to contribute.

We hope that you go forth in this work and know that you are appreciated, valued, and loved.

LEARNING MORE

Here, we provide resources to help you learn more about taking care of yourself and connecting with others as you pursue systems-level justice work or social action. Several resources listed in this appendix cover multiple topics in this book—for example, the website for the Beck Institute for Cognitive Behavior Therapy addresses a number of topics that may be of interest. And if you are interested in guides for therapists and separate workbooks for clients, check out Oxford Clinical Psychology's *Treatments That Work*, an Oxford University Press book series addressing an assortment of subjects.

Also available are a myriad of apps on psychological topics. A word of caution: Apps that purport to be about mental health topics are not necessarily created by (or even in consultation with) mental health professionals. As a result, these apps vary widely in quality (for more on this topic, see the article "Mental Wellness Apps Are Basically the Wild West of Therapy" at https://www.popsci.com/science/mental-health-apps-safety/). Mental wellness apps can be enormously helpful tools, and we are thrilled that the technology we use for so many other things is being harnessed to promote psychological health.

A few we particularly like are MoodKit, Calm, Headspace, and Insight Timer. However, we encourage you to do some research on apps before buying or using them. New apps appear all the time, so you'll want to check out any you are considering by reading reviews at sites, such as the following:

- One Mind PsyberGuide: https://onemindpsyberguide.org/
- Mind M-Health Index & Navigation Database: https://mindapps.org/
- American Psychological Association Division 56, Trauma Psychology: https://www.apatraumadivision.org/606/mental-health-app-database.html

If you are considering beginning psychotherapy, you might wish to ask your doctor or other health care provider for recommendations. You can also find therapists near you at websites such as the following:

- Psychology Today: https://www.psychologytoday.com/us
- Mental Health Match: https://mentalhealthmatch.com/

These services allow you to search by insurance provider. You may also wish to contact your insurance provider or employee assistance program directly, regarding referrals.

If you are looking specifically for a therapist who uses research-based treatment strategies, you might consider this therapist directory:

- Association of Behavioral and Cognitive Therapies: https://services.abct.org/i4a/memberDirectory/index.cfm?directory_id=3&pageID=3282 (note that these therapists may or may not take insurance)

The Substance Abuse and Mental Health Services Administration also runs a helpline. For information about and referrals for treatment online, visit https://www.samhsa.gov/find-help/national-helpline or call 1-800-662-HELP (4357).

MORE RESOURCES, BY TOPIC

In this section, we list other specific resources, organized by topic.

Acceptance and Commitment Therapy, or ACT

- Association for Contextual Behavioral Science: https://contextualscience.org/act

Harris, R. (2019). *ACT made simple: An easy-to-read primer on acceptance and commitment therapy.* New Harbinger Publications.

Hayes, S. C. (2005). *Get out of your mind and into your life: The new acceptance and commitment therapy.* New Harbinger Publications.

Anxiety and Relaxation

- Diaphragmatic breathing exercise from the University of California, Irvine: https://ssihi.uci.edu/tip/breathing-exercises-for-stress-relief-audio-exercises/
- Progressive muscle relaxation exercise from Anxiety Canada: https://www.anxietycanada.com/articles/how-to-do-progressive-muscle-relaxation/?fbclid=IwAR3RTFA-rser-v9hsPIdcDCpy43W_Ern-MeNLQjxd8JKTjGjDbYDTJCCmP4

Bourne, E. J. (2020). *The anxiety and phobia workbook* (4th ed.). New Harbinger Publications.

Davis, M., Eshelman, E. R., & McKay, M. (2008). *The relaxation and stress reduction workbook* (6th ed.). New Harbinger Publications.

Harris, D. (2019). *10% Happier: How I tamed the voice in my head, reduced stress without losing my edge, and found self-help that actually works— A true story.* Yellow Kite.

Character Strengths

- VIA Institute on Character survey: https://www.viacharacter.org/survey/surveys/takesurvey

Seligman, M. E. P. (2004). *Authentic happiness: Using the new positive psychology to realize your potential for lasting fulfillment.* Atria Books.
Seligman, M. E. P. (2012). *Flourish: A visionary new understanding of happiness and well-being.* Atria Books.

Cognitive Behavior Therapy, or CBT

- Cognitive model from the Beck Institute for Cognitive Behavior Therapy: https://beckinstitute.org/cognitive-model/
- Cognitive reappraisal from the Harvard University Stress & Development Lab: https://sdlab.fas.harvard.edu/cognitive-reappraisal/identifying-negative-automatic-thought-patterns
- Association for Behavioral and Cognitive Therapies: https://www.abct.org

Communication and Boundaries

Kim, A. S., & Del Prado, A. (2019). *It's time to talk (and listen): How to have constructive conversations about race, class, sexuality, ability and gender in a polarized world.* New Harbinger Publications.
Tawwab, N. G. (2021). *Set boundaries, find peace: A guide to reclaiming yourself.* Penguin Random House.

Compassion and Self-Compassion

- Compassion It: https://compassionit.com/
- Kristin Neff's self-compassion website: https://self-compassion.org/

- Stanford Medicine, The Center for Compassion and Altruism Research and Education: http://ccare.stanford.edu/

Neff, K. (2011). *Self-compassion: The proven power of being kind to yourself.* Hachette UK.

Neff, K. (2021). *Fierce self-compassion: How women can harness kindness to speak up, claim their power, and thrive.* Penguin Life.

Neff, K., & Germer, C. K. (2018). *The mindful self-compassion workbook: A proven way to accept yourself, build inner strength, and thrive.* Guilford Press.

Schairer, S. (2021, March 22). *What's the difference between empathy, sympathy, and compassion?* Chopra. https://chopra.com/articles/whats-the-difference-between-empathy-sympathy-and-compassion.

Connecting With Others

- Meetup: https://www.meetup.com/
- Mental health support from Active Minds: https://www.activeminds.org
- For those affected by mental illness, from the National Alliance on Mental Illness: https://www.nami.org/Home
- Idealist.org's mutual aid group locator database information and link: https://www.idealist.org/en/days/what-is-a-mutual-aid-network

Fitch, B. (2010). *Citizen's handbook to influencing elected officials: Citizen advocacy in state legislatures and Congress—A guide for citizen lobbyists and grassroots advocates.* The CapitolNet.

Dialectical Behavior Therapy

- DialecticalBehaviorTherapy.com: https://dialecticalbehaviortherapy.com/
- Behavioral Tech: https://behavioraltech.org

Distress Tolerance (see *Dialectical Behavior Therapy*)

Forest Bathing (see *Mindfulness and Meditation*)

Growth Mindset

- Growth Mindset Institute: https://www.growthmindsetinstitute.org
- Khan Academy: https://www.khanacademy.org/college-careers-more/talks-and-interviews/talks-and-interviews-unit/conversations-with-sal/a/the-learning-myth-why-ill-never-tell-my-son-hes-smart
- *The Atlantic* article "How Praise Became a Consolation Prize": https://www.theatlantic.com/education/archive/2016/12/how-praise-became-a-consolation-prize/510845/

Dweck, C. S. (2017). *Mindset: Changing the way you think to fulfill your potential*. Robinson.

Implementation Intentions (see *Productivity*)

Interpersonal Effectiveness (see *Dialectical Behavior Therapy*)

Mindfulness and Meditation

- Omega Institute for Holistic Studies: https://www.eomega.org
- Tara Brach: https://www.tarabrach.com/
- Compassion It: https://compassionit.com
- UMass Memorial Health, Center for Mindfulness's mindfulness-based stress reduction, or MBSR, training program: https://www.ummhealth.org/umass-memorial-medical-center/services-treatments/center-for-mindfulness/mindfulness-classes

Gunaratana, B. H. (2019). *Mindfulness in plain English*. Wisdom Publications.
Kabat-Zinn, J. (2013). *Full catastrophe living: Using the wisdom of your body and mind to face stress, pain, and illness*. Bantam Books.

Li, Q. (2018). *Forest bathing: How trees can help you find health and happiness.* Viking.

Magee, R. V., & Kabat-Zinn, J. (2021). *The inner work of racial justice: Healing ourselves and transforming our communities through mindfulness.* TarcherPerigee.

Salzburg, S. (2020). *Real change: Mindfulness to heal ourselves and the world.* Flatiron books.

Wright, R. (2018). *Why Buddhism is true: The science and philosophy of meditation and enlightenment.* Simon & Schuster.

Physical Activity

- *The Guardian* article "How to Stay Fit Forever: 25 Tips to Keep Moving When Life Gets in the Way": https://www.theguardian.com/lifeandstyle/2018/sep/12/how-to-stay-fit-for-ever-25-tips-keep-exercising-expert-advice
- Live Science article "Short Bouts of Exercise Benefit Health, Too": https://www.livescience.com/26772-short-exercise-bouts-benefit-health.html

Productivity

- American Psychological Association article "Boosting Productivity" in *Monitor on Psychology*: https://www.apa.org/monitor/2017/09/boosting-productivity
- Medium blog post in *Human Parts*: "Laziness Does Not Exist: But Unseen Barriers Do": https://humanparts.medium.com/laziness-does-not-exist-3af27e312d01
- *Greater Good Magazine* article "The Three Most Important Tactics for Keeping Your Resolutions": https://greatergood.berkeley.edu/article/item/the_three_most_important_tactics_for_keeping_your_resolutions

McGonigal, K. (2012). *The willpower instinct: How self-control works, why it matters, and what you can do to get more of it.* Avery.

Pinsker, J. (2021, August 11). The best time-management advice is depressing but liberating. *The Atlantic.* https://www.theatlantic.com/family/archive/2021/08/oliver-burkeman-advice-time-productivity/619723/

Self-Soothing (see *Dialectical Behavior Therapy***)**

Sleep

- National Institutes of Health article "The Benefits of Slumber: Why You Need a Good Night's Sleep" in *NIH News in Health*: https://newsinhealth.nih.gov/2013/04/benefits-slumber
- *The Atlantic* article "Listen: You Are Worthy of Sleep": https://www.theatlantic.com/health/archive/2020/04/you-are-worthy-of-sleep/610996/

Walker, M. (2018). *Why we sleep: Unlocking the power of sleep and dreams.* Scribner.

REFERENCES

A few of the sources listed in this section are not cited directly in the text. We wanted to give credit, though, to these sources from which we synthesized information for the book and others that inspired stories and examples in the book.

Abrams, S. (2018). *Minority leader: How to lead from the outside and make real change.* Henry Holt and Company.

Abrams, S. (2020). *Our time is now: Power, purpose, and the fight for a fair America.* Henry Holt and Company.

Americans With Disabilities Act of 1990, Pub. L. 101–336, 42 U.S.C. §§ 12101–12213 (2000).

Bandura, A. (2011). Una perspectiva social cognitiva de la psicología positive [A social cognitive perspective on positive psychology]. *Revista de Psicología Social* [*International Journal of Social Psychology*], 26(1), 7–20. https://doi.org/10.1174/021347411794078444

Beck Institute. (n.d.). *Introduction to CBT.* https://beckinstitute.org/about/intro-to-cbt

Beck, J. S. (2021). *Cognitive behavior therapy: Basics and beyond* (3rd ed.). Guilford Press.

Brown, A. C. (2018). *I'm still here: Black dignity in a world made for Whiteness.* Convergent Books.

Buchanan, L., Bui, Q., & Patel, J. K. (2020, July 3). Black Lives Matter may be the largest movement in U.S. history. *The New York Times.* https://

www.nytimes.com/interactive/2020/07/03/us/george-floyd-protests-crowd-size.html

Burkeman, O. (2021). *Four thousand weeks: Time management for mortals.* Farrar, Straus and Giroux.

Cherry, M. (2021). *The case for rage: Why anger is essential to anti-racist struggle.* Oxford University Press.

Durant, W. (1961). *The story of philosophy: The lives and opinions of the world's greatest philosophers of the Western world.* Simon & Schuster Paperbacks.

Ellis, A. (1987). A sadly neglected cognitive element in depression. *Cognitive Therapy and Research, 11*(1), 121–145. https://doi.org/10.1007/BF01183137

Frank, A. (2008). *Anne Frank's tales from the secret annex: A collection of her short stories, fables, and lesser-known writings* (S. Massotty, Trans.; Rev. ed.). Bantam. (From original work written in Frank's notebook between 1943 and 1944)

Harper's Bazaar Staff. (2017, May 22). 21 of Maya Angelou's best quotes to inspire. *Harper's Bazaar.* https://www.harpersbazaar.com/culture/features/a9874244/best-maya-angelou-quotes/

Hayes, S. (n.d.). *ACT.* Association for Contextual Behavioral Science. https://contextualscience.org/act

Hayes, S. C. (2019). *A liberated mind: How to pivot toward what matters.* Avery.

Hayes, S. C., Strosahl, K. D., & Wilson, K. G. (2012). *Acceptance and commitment therapy: The process and practice of mindful change* (2nd ed.). Guilford Press.

Hofstrand, D. (2016, August). *Vision and mission statements—A roadmap of where you want to go and how to get there.* Iowa State University Extension and Outreach. https://www.extension.iastate.edu/agdm/wholefarm/html/c5-09.html

hooks, b. (2018). *All about love: New visions.* William Morrow.

James, W. (1890). *The principles of psychology.* H. Holt and Company.

Kabat-Zinn, J. (2005). *Full catastrophe living: Using the wisdom of your body and mind to face stress, pain, and illness* (15th Anniv. ed.). Delta Trade Paperbacks.

Kendi, I. X. (2019). *How to be an antiracist.* One World.

Linehan, M. M. (1997). Validation and psychotherapy. In A. C. Bohart & L. S. Greenberg (Eds.), *Empathy reconsidered: New directions in psychotherapy* (pp. 353–392). American Psychological Association.

Linehan, M. M. (2014). *DBT skills training manual* (2nd ed.). Guilford Press.

Lorde, A. (2020). *The selected works of Audre Lorde* (R. Gay, Ed.). W. W. Norton & Company.

Merriam-Webster. (n.d.). Activism. In *Merriam-Webster.com dictionary*. Retrieved May 2, 2022, from https://www.merriam-webster.com/dictionary/activism

Miller, W. R., & Rollnick, S. (2013). *Motivational interviewing: Helping people change* (3rd ed.). Guilford Press.

Moraga, C., & Anzaldúa, G. (Eds.). (2015). *This bridge called my back: Writings by radical women of color* (4th ed.). SUNY Press.

Morton, B. (2011, August 11). Falser words were never spoken [Opinion]. *The New York Times*. https://www.nytimes.com/2011/08/30/opinion/falser-words-were-never-spoken.html

Muñoz, R. F., Ippen, C. G., Rao, S., Le, H.-N., & Dwyer, E. V. (2020, May). *Manual for group cognitive-behavioral therapy of major depression: A reality management approach* [Participant manual]. University of California, San Francisco. https://i4health.paloaltou.edu/downloads/CBT_Participant_English.pdf

Neff, K. (2021). *Fierce self-compassion: How women can harness kindness to speak up, claim their power, and thrive*. Penguin Life.

Obama Foundation. (2021, May 26). *My Brother's Keeper Alliance Leadership forum: A conversation with President Obama* [Video]. https://www.obama.org/video/lf-obama/

Peterson, C., & Seligman, M. E. P. (2004). *Character strengths and virtues: A handbook and classification*. American Psychological Association; Oxford University Press.

Prochaska, J. O., & DiClemente, C. C. (1983). Stages and processes of self-change of smoking: Toward an integrative model of change. *Journal of Consulting and Clinical Psychology, 51*(3), 390–395. https://doi.org/10.1037/0022-006X.51.3.390

Prochaska, J. O., DiClemente, C. C., & Norcross, J. C. (1992). In search of how people change: Applications to addictive behaviors. *American Psychologist, 47*(9), 1102–1114. https://doi.org/10.1037/0003-066X.47.9.1102

Steinem, G. (2019). *The truth will set you free, but first it will piss you off: Thoughts on life, love, and rebellion.* Random House.

Stress & Development Lab. (n.d.). *Identifying negative automatic thought patterns.* Harvard University. https://sdlab.fas.harvard.edu/cognitive-reappraisal/identifying-negative-automatic-thought-patterns

Tawwab, N. G. (2021). *Set boundaries, find peace: A guide to reclaiming yourself.* Penguin Random House.

Urbaniak, K. (2020). *Unbound: A woman's guide to power.* TarcherPerigee.

Vaccaro, A., & Mena, J. A. (2011). It's not burnout, it's more: Queer college activists of color and mental health. *Journal of Gay & Lesbian Mental Health, 15*(4), 339–367. https://doi.org/10.1080/19359705.2011.600656

VIA Institute on Character. (n.d.). *The VIA Character Strengths Survey: Get to know your greatest strengths.* https://www.viacharacter.org/account/register

Vivyan, C. (2010). *Thought record sheet.* Getselfhelp.co.uk. https://www.getselfhelp.co.uk/docs/ThoughtRecordSheet7.pdf

Wasik, S. (2018, February 7). *Fighting for a better world: Heather Booth on the power of organization and activism.* The University of Chicago Institute of Politics. http://uchicagogate.com/articles/2018/2/7/h/

Willcox, G. (1982). The Feeling Wheel: A tool for expanding awareness of emotions and increasing spontaneity and intimacy. *Transactional Analysis Journal, 12*(4), 274–276. https://doi.org/10.1177/036215378201200411

Wright, R. (2018). *Why Buddhism is true: The science and philosophy of meditation and enlightenment.* Simon & Schuster.

INDEX

ABOUT THE AUTHORS

Dara G. Friedman-Wheeler, PhD, is a licensed clinical psychologist in Maryland and a research psychologist at the Suicide Care, Prevention, and Research Initiative at Uniformed Services University of the Health Sciences in Bethesda, Maryland. She is on the speakers' faculty of the Beck Institute for Cognitive Behavior Therapy in Philadelphia, Pennsylvania.

Dr. Friedman-Wheeler earned her undergraduate degree at Vassar College in Poughkeepsie, New York, and her master's and PhD degrees in clinical psychology from American University in Washington, DC. She completed a 2-year fellowship (internship and postdoctoral fellowship) at the University of California, San Francisco, where she focused on community mental health and behavioral medicine in her work in a primary care liaison clinic, psychiatric emergency services, and an inpatient unit. She went on to complete an additional year of postdoctoral training with Aaron T. Beck at the Aaron T. Beck Psychopathology Research Unit at the University of Pennsylvania before joining the faculty at Goucher College in Baltimore, where she taught for 13 years, and then working at the Center for Psychedelic and Consciousness Research at The Johns Hopkins University School of Medicine.

In addition to her research role at Uniformed Services University, she has a small private practice. She also conducts workshops on "taking care of yourself while taking care of the world" for those doing work in social justice or advocacy fields.

Jamie S. Bodenlos, PhD, is a licensed clinical psychologist in New York and a professor of psychological science at Hobart and William Smith Colleges in Geneva, New York. She is a fellow at the Society of Behavioral Medicine.

Dr. Bodenlos earned a bachelor's degree in psychology from the University of Pittsburgh and a master's degree in clinical psychology from Western Carolina University in Cullowhee, North Carolina. She completed a PhD in clinical psychology at Louisiana State University in Baton Rouge and a 1-year internship at the Medical University of South Carolina in Charleston. For 3 years, she worked as a postdoctoral research fellow at the University of Massachusetts Chan Medical School in Worcester.

She has authored 47 peer-reviewed journal articles in the areas of behavioral medicine, mindfulness, and health behaviors. She teaches courses in cognitive behavior therapy, clinical psychology, and behavioral medicine. She presents on the topic of science activism and communication at professional conferences and has a webinar on writing op-eds for the field of behavioral medicine. In addition to scholarship and teaching, Dr. Bodenlos also uses cognitive behavior techniques in clinical work she does in the community.